The Last Grizzly

The Last Grizzly

and Other Southwestern
Bear Stories

compiled by David E. Brown
and John A. Murray

The University of Arizona Press, Tucson

The University of Arizona Press
www.uapress.arizona.edu

© 1988 The Arizona Board of Regents
All rights reserved. Published 1988
First paperback edition 2014

Printed in the United States of America
19 18 17 16 15 14   6 5 4 3 2

ISBN-13: 978-0-8165-1067-2 (cloth)
ISBN-13: 978-0-8165-0123-6 (paper)

Cover Photo: Grizzly bear on a rock overlooking by Erwin and
Peggy Bauer, U.S. Fish and Wildlife Service
Cover design by Miriam Warren

Frontis: Young grizzly killed on the Nail Ranch homestead, Gila
County, Arizona, about 1905. Photograph courtesy of Nathan
Ellison.

Library of Congress Cataloging-in-Publication Data
The Last grizzly and other Southwestern bear stories / compiled by
    David E. Brown and John A. Murray
        p. cm.
    ISBN 0-8165-1067-9 (alk. paper)
    1. Grizzly bear. 2. Bear hunting—Southwestern States.
3. Mammals—Southwestern States. I. Brown, David E. (David Earl),
1938– . II. Murray, John A., 1954- .
QL737.C27L385   1988
599.74'446—dc19   88-14819
                                                         CIP

♾ This paper meets the requirements of ANSI/NISO Z39.48-1992
(Permanence of Paper).

Contents

Introduction

A citizen of Clifton writes to her local paper that Wm. Sparks, better known as "Timberline," had a lively time with a bear. . . . Mr. Sparks had set a trap for a mountain lion and on visiting it found that a bear had been caught and walked off with the whole outfit. He started in pursuit with a Winchester. . . . when he did find him, bruin was mad and in stepping back to avoid an infuriated rush, Timberline fell, face under, down hill. The bear lost no time taking advantage of the situation and seizing Timberline . . . gave him a lively shaking up. The victim of this rough usage however held fast to his rifle and managed . . . to fire a ball that entered the bear's mouth and this ended the battle. . . .

Arizona Daily Star, June 14, 1888

Wherever bears and man have coexisted, their contacts have been immortalized in oral legend and written word. Humankind's fascination with the genus *Ursus* antedates civilization, extending well back into the Pleistocene. Near Erd, Hungary, there is a cave in which Neanderthals ritually placed a large number of bear skulls 50,000 years ago. Between 30,000 and 10,000 years ago, Paleolithic peoples painted bears on cave walls and continued to place bear skulls in ceremonial niches. These ancient peoples worshiped the now extinct cave bear in what may have been a bear-mother or bear-son cult. Bears were considered both relatives and spiritual beings.

Bear ceremonials, besides being ancient, intercontinental and boreal, appear to have a common Old World origin. The bear, like nature, temporarily "dies"—goes into hibernation in winter—and is then reborn in spring. The bear is a special being: humanlike, yet belonging to a pristine, natural world.

Bear worship persists into modern times. In 1690 Henry Kelsey, exploring the Canadian prairie for the Hudson's Bay Company, killed a grizzly bear and ate a portion of its meat. The Indians, however, urged him not to keep the skin, because, in Kelsey's words, "They said it was God." In a contemporary legend in Mexico's Sierra Madre Occidental, a woman bred by a bear gives birth to a man-bear, Juan Oso. As late as the 1960s, the Ainu of Hokkaido, Japan, practiced the Ioymande ritual, in which a bear was ritually slain and offered to the mountain god to attest to the purity of its captivity and death. In the Southwest, bear ceremonialism is, or was until very recently, practiced by the Navajo, Ute, Apache, and Tarahumara Indians.

Bear legends consist of more than simple recollections of hunting prowess, slaughter, and celebration. Bears resonate with a multitude of associations, religious and archetypal, ritualistic and heroic, ancient and modern. Almost all bear stories have a pronounced, if unintentional, mythological quality, and they achieve a catharsis. Beneath a surface narrative of lore, suffering and gore, triumph and trophy, there is another world, a symbolic realm in which the hunt assumes the import of a religious quest. A bear, as William Faulkner wrote in his novel, *The Bear*, is not

a mortal beast but an anachronism indomitable and invincible out of an old, dead time, a phantom, epitome, and apotheosis of the old wild life.

Not merely yarns or episodic adventure narratives, bear stories speak to the timeless battle between the human race and nature, and to the bear's singular status as nature's supreme symbol in the Northern Hemisphere. The bear is not only the nemesis of the stockman, beekeeper, and camper, he is the preeminent carnivore, the local embodiment of *terra incognita*, the visible reminder of the disturbing powers that defy and outlast us. And, too, those who dare to kill a god, may become one themselves. The successful hunt that once initiated manhood or secured clan power still inspires awe and elicits envy.

Bear stories, like cowboys, Indians, and lost mines are an integral ingredient of our Southwest heritage. The literature is rife with stories of bear fights, many of which are retold and embellished around the campfire. No wonder then that some of the best tales find themselves perpetuated not only in print but on canvas and in bronze. Like the prefacing account, the full story of which is told in William ("Timberline Bill") Sparks's book *A Bear Fight and Other Stories*, the bruin involved is almost invariably a grizzly. No other Southwest animal evoked such wonder—a reverence now held only in memory.

The outcome of most "bear stories" is monotonously familiar. Another bear death is added to the litany of conquests. Yet, the appeal of these tales cannot be denied. Perhaps we believe that by vicariously reliving these accounts, we can recreate the great beast's presence. And so we can; for such is the wonder of imagination and the treasure of the written word. A good thing, for that is about all we have left. There are today only a tiny few who have met a Southwest grizzly.

What is it about the grizzly that fascinates us so? Certainly, his size and ferocity, that he was, as the pioneer naturalist E. A. Mearns noted, "the largest game found in this region with the exception of the elk. . . ," has something to do with it. The fact that no other Southwest animal disputed man's encroachment is also a factor, as is their individual personality. Like the wolf and unlike the mountain lion, the grizzly had character. Individual silvertips were identifiable, and as such were celebrated; some, such as "Susie" and the "Wiseman Grizzly" described herein, became locally famous.

Like so many boys, we grew up reading the stories of the West. Bears, being wild creatures and not tamed by the civilization that demeaned the idealized western man of our youth, retained their fascination. Bears, even if only the less awesome black bear, symbolized the wildness of the wilderness. When we lost the grizzly, we lost more than a symbol of the frontier; we lost its representative.

Not much remains of the Southwest's grizzlies; a mounted specimen or two, a few skins, a tiny collection of faded photos, and a legacy of stories. Any real knowledge of Southwest grizzlies can only be obtained from the written word. Newspaper accounts, old letters, and hurried jottings in journals are our only remembrances. For these reasons accurate information is hard to come by.

Nor has it been easy putting the last grizzlies to rest. In Arizona it was thought that the state's *last* grizzly had been properly documented—September 13, 1935. Although other grizzlies were said to accompany the one slain, there were no subsequent mentions of grizzlies in the literature. Or so we thought.

While poring through old federal-aid reports on turkeys, the senior editor found this startling entry by Lynn L. Hargrave:

One grizzly bear, an immature, was killed by Polk on the northwest slope of Mount Baldy, White Mountains, Fort Apache Indian Reservation during the summer of 1939.

The report went on to state that other grizzlies had been run by dogs and seen that year, both on the Reservation and in the adjacent Blue Range. The U.S. trapper working on the Fort Apache Indian Reservation, B. B. Polk, was credited with taking 103 black bears between May 5 and November 25, 1939, but the Biological Survey's state report for that year makes no mention of grizzlies on the Reservation. The men responsible for killing off these wonderful animals were already conscious of their crime and covering their tracks. This long forgotten report by a state contract biologist was an "aside" for the historical record. Otherwise, Arizona's "last griz" would have been expunged from the written record in true Orwellian style. Others undoubtedly were.

The date of New Mexico's last grizzly of record is also open to question. Although the last published accounts of New Mexican silvertips are from the Black Range in 1930 and near Alma in 1931, there appear to have been even later records. A skull in the U. S. National Museum from Magdalena Baldy is dated 1935.

As recently as 1979, after a hiatus of more than 20 years, a female grizzly appeared in Colorado's San Juan Mountains to administer one more provoked mauling before passing on to become a state's last grizzly of record. Even though there hasn't been an authenticated record of a grizzly in Mexico for more than 25 years, rumors of "*oso grande*" holding out in some remote region of the Sierra Madre are about as easy to dispel as to persuade a Crusader that the Holy Grail was irretrievably lost.

To understand this conflict, we have selected a series of representative articles on southwestern bear encounters. Although many of the stories we have included are entertaining and represent some well-told tales, we have omitted questionable and obviously exaggerated accounts, no matter how well written they may be. To maintain as much veracity as possible, we have regretfully abstained from using the rich literature of native and Hispanic peoples passed down through oral legend. Also not included are accounts only recently published. Accordingly, with the exception of "Bear Cosper and Fred Fritz's Bear Fights," we do not include those stories contained in *The Grizzly Bear: Portraits from Life*, edited by B. D. and E. Haynes, and *The Grizzly Bear in the Southwest* by Dave Brown, both presently in press with the University of Oklahoma Press.

Our "Southwest" takes in the states of Arizona, New Mexico, Colorado, Utah, Chihuahua, Sonora, and Southern California. The time frame is from the arrival of Anglo-Americans in the 1820s to the present, thus spanning the period from "Westering Man's" initial encounters with the Great Bear to his eventual and absolute victory— a feat that, once attained, was never celebrated; only the conflict would be cherished.

The stories have been selected for their instructive lessons and are divided into four broad categories, each representing a general period in the history of Western Man's interactions with Southwest bears. A gradual change in attitude is noted in the participants. The challenge of battling a formidable foe in a new land shines through the earlier narratives of mountain men, a natural history collector, British remittance men, and a self-taught naturalist. The second series of stories is "grisly reading" in the truest sense, as we learn the physical price paid by settlers to dislodge the grizzly from his domain—a cost that makes the idea of reintroducing grizzlies to the Southwest anathema to pioneer cattlemen and many of their descendants. Next we are treated to the self-righteous justifications of professional hunters and stockmen as they seek to punish "renegade" holdouts before or after the bears have committed livestock depredations. Finally, we are left with the wistful expectations of those seeking bears after the grizzly is gone, or nearly so. Not surprisingly, three of the stories in this section involve "last grizzlies," and the remainder are about black bears. These later celebrations of the grizzly's more adaptable cousin reflect the spirit, if not the presence, of the Great Bear and are a reminder of how fortunate we are that at least one of the two species of bear survives and prospers.

The history of the black bear in the Southwest is, in contrast with the grizzly, one of gradual accommodation and eventual replenishment. Although both species of bear were persecuted through the settlement years and even into the 1940s, the more numerous black bear survived to benefit from the emerging conservation ethic of the 1920s. The bear's belated status as game and a slightly higher reproductive rate prevented widespread extirpation. Today the bear has made a remarkable comeback and, except for Mexico and a few isolated mountain ranges, this bruin has regained most of his ancestoral haunts.

Not so the grizzly. His irascibility and refusal to starve on overgrazed ranges made him the victim of ranchers' vengeance and government policy. But the men who killed these bears were victims too, as were we who came to inherit a Southwest without them. Like Melville's Captain Ahab and Moby Dick, these men slayed the beast but also paid a price in return. And, as Ishmael lives to carry the story of the white whale back to civilization, so do Hyrum Naegle's brother George and the other narrators relate the story of our loss.

To restore the grizzly to the Southwest will be to complete a job begun by President Theodore Roosevelt and Aldo Leopold when they envisioned a system of Forest Reserves and wilderness to perpetuate America's frontier spirit. To ensure the survival of both bears is the task of our and future generations. Until such time as political coalitions to reintroduce grizzlies are forged, programs funded, and grizzlies released, we will have to be content with stories from the past. But read these tales with the hope that one day, somewhere in the Southwest, you may one day see, in a grassy clearing, high above the trail, one of those legendary frosted coats lumbering off into the aspens.

In the meantime, learn of the grizzly's character, the methods used to exterminate him, and the character and thought processes of the men who participated in his destruction. You will also become more aware of the difficulties of frontier life.

A word of caution, however. The natural histories of both grizzly and black bears were imperfectly known as recently as the 1960s. Then improved capture devices and radio tracking equipment greatly accelerated the scientific study of bears—but long after Southwest grizzlies had been reduced to all but a memory and after most of the accounts contained herein were written. Although selected on the basis of their general veracity and informed content, many of the stories contain interpretive statements that need not always be taken at face value. Tooker's description of a pair of mated bears at a time when the female had young in the den is almost certainly in error. Other sightings, such as the large numbers of bears seen in one place by Dyche, while possible, would be an unusual event in the Sangre de Cristos. His, and other reports of multiple bears, either indicate community feeding on a temporarily abundant food source, a tolerance behavior different from that recorded by more recent observers, or exaggerated embellishment.

Some will find the repetitious killing offensive. Such is perhaps as it should be. But then, is it not also the bear hunters among us who yearn for the grizzly the most? It is only a perceived irony that the organization most actively engaged in projects to benefit black bears and promote the idea of reintroducing grizzlies to the Southwest is the The Arizona Bear Society, a 300+ member organization founded by bear hunters. But then in the annals of North American conservation history it has always been hunters who promulgated the most meaningful attempts at wildlife restoration.

Not all the stories are bloody and tragic. Nat Straw's hilarious tale of his "tame" grizzly, *Geronimo*, which first appeared in "Golden Liars of the Golden West," published by *Vanity Fair* in 1931, is representative of another kind of bear story: the outrageous. Humor was a distinctive aspect of the frontier, and no anthology of bear stories would be complete without at least one selection from this enjoyable body of literature. Without laughter, the grinding hardships of adversity and loneliness would have made frontier life unbearable.

Enjoy reading about the bears of your lost past; revel in the adventure that was, and learn the lore of Southwest grizzlies. There may not be any more stories to tell.

PART I

Hunting Bears for Fun and Profit

The Age of Discovery, 1826–1890

Duett Ellison and grizzly taken in central Arizona Territory just after the turn of the century. Photograph courtesy of the Arizona Historical Foundation, Hayden University Library, Tempe, Arizona.

Killing a Grizzly in Its Den

James Ohio Pattie

ca. 1826

Pattie was one of the first Anglo-Americans to explore the Southwest, arriving in Mexico's Santa Fe in November 1825. His *Personal Narrative of James Ohio Pattie of Kentucky*, edited by Timothy Flint and published in 1833 by John H. Wood of Cincinnati, after he returned from his adventures, is one of the primary sources on the American fur trade in the Southwest. In it, Pattie chronicled his extraordinary travels through present-day Kansas, Colorado, New Mexico, Arizona, and California. While scholars have disputed the veracity of his recollections, particularly his hopelessly muddled chronology, there is little doubt that the young mountain man had numerous adventures in a wild region and that he could tell a story with the best of them.[1]

In this passage, Pattie describes an incident that occurred on the upper Gila River on January 25, 1826, in or near the present Gila Wilderness Area. Coming upon what was presumably a grizzly bear

[1] For a summary of Pattie's travels in Arizona and comment on his contributions to the discovery of the region's natural history, the reader is referred to Goode P. Davis's *Man and Wildlife in Arizona*, edited by Neil B. Carmony and David E. Brown, published by the Arizona Game and Fish Department in 1982 and republished in 1986. Richard Batman in his *James Pattie's West: The Dream and the Reality* (University of Oklahoma Press, 1984) gives an excellent description and analysis of Pattie's travels throughout the West.

den along the river, Pattie proceeded to enter the natural cave and dispatch the bear with his rifle. Earlier in his narrative he describes other encounters with "white bears" on the divide between the Platte and Arkansas rivers, in what is today eastern Colorado. This incident, the first Anglo account of a bear encounter in the Southwest, is ominous in that it portends the eventual fate of the grizzly once the region was occupied. Pattie's cavalier attitude toward the bear illustrates the psyche of a growing number of frontiersmen that would forever alter the West. 🐾

In the evening of the same day, although the weather threatened a storm, we packed up, and began to descend the river. We encamped this night in a huge cavern in the midst of the rocks. About night it began to blow a tempest, and to snow fast. Our horses became impatient under the pelting of the storm, broke their ropes, and disappeared. In the morning, the earth was covered with snow, four or five inches deep. One of our companions accompanied me to search for our horses. We soon came upon their trail, and followed it, until it crossed the river. We found it on the opposite side, and pursued it up a creek, that empties into the Helay [Gila River] on the north shore. We passed a cave at the foot of the cliffs. At its mouth I remarked, that the bushes were beaten down, as though some animal had been browsing upon them. I was aware, that a bear had entered the cave. We collected some pine knots, split them with our tomahawks, and kindled torches, with which I proposed to my companion, that we should enter the cave, and shoot the bear. He gave me a decided refusal, notwithstanding I reminded him, that I had, more than once, stood by him in a similar adventure; and notwithstanding I made him sensible, that a bear in a den is by no means so formidable, as when ranging freely in the woods. Finding it impossible to prevail on him to accompany me, I lashed my torch to a stick, and placed it parallel with the gun barrel, so as that I could see the sights on it, and entered the cave. I advanced cautiously onward about twenty yards, seeing nothing. On a sudden the bear reared himself erect within seven feet of me, and began to growl, and gnash his teeth. I levelled my gun and shot him between the eyes, and began to retreat. Whatever light it may throw upon my courage, I admit, that I was in such a hurry, as to stumble, and extinguish my light. The growling and struggling of the bear did not at all contribute to allay my apprehensions. On the contrary, I was in such haste to get out of the dark place, thinking the bear just at my heels, that I fell several times on the rocks, by which I cut my limbs, and lost my gun. When I reached the light, my companion declared, and I can believe it, that I was as pale as a corpse. It was sometime, before I could summon sufficient courage to re-enter the cavern for my gun. But having re-kindled my light, and borrowed my companions gun, I entered the cavern again, advanced and listened. All was silent, and I advanced still further, and found my gun, near where I had shot the bear. Here again I paused and listened. I then advanced onward a few strides, where to my great joy I found the animal dead. I returned, and brought my companion in with me. We attempted to drag the carcass from the den, but so great was the size, that we found ourselves wholly unable. We went out, found our horses, and returned to camp for assistance. My father severely reprimanded me for venturing to attack such a dangerous animal in its den, when the failure to kill it outright by the first shot, would have been sure to be followed by my death.

Four of us were detached to the den. We were soon enabled to drag the bear to the light, and by the aid of our beasts to take it to camp. It was both the largest and whitest bear I ever saw. The best proof, I can give, of the size and fatness is, that we extracted ten gallons of oil from it. The meat we dried, and put the oil in a trough, which we secured in a deep crevice of a cliff, beyond the reach of animals of prey. We were sensible that it would prove a treasure to us on our return.

A Convention of Grizzlies

Dick Wootton

ca. 1850

"Uncle Dick" Wootton was one of the infamous mountain men of America's pre–Civil War West and a companion of such notable frontiersmen as Kit Carson and Old Jim Baker. Born in Virginia and raised in Kentucky, Wootton headed west from Independence, Missouri, as a wagoner at age 19. Lured by the frontier life and the promise of quick profit from beaver pelts, young Wootton dropped out of the wagon train at Bent's Fort in southeastern Colorado to lead a fur-trapping expedition into the Rockies. From then on the Rocky Mountain West was his home, and he became in turn a trapper, trader, scout, guide, Indian fighter, buffalo hunter, rancher, stagecoach station operator, and innkeeper.

His recollections, from which the following passages were taken, were written down by H. L. Conrad and published in 1890 under the title *"Uncle Dick" Wootton: The Pioneer Frontiersman of the Rocky Mountain Region*, by W. E. Dibble and Co. of Chicago. What makes Wootton's reminiscences valuable are his first-hand descriptions of the frontier and his having seen grizzlies go from "a great many" to "rarely heard of." And Wootton, who operated mostly in the Cimarron Mountains area along the Colorado–New Mexico border north of Raton, knew grizzlies well. Although he killed his share, he never got over his admiration and respect for the Great Bear. Like most frontiersmen, he considered the grizzly generally to be ferocious only when on the defensive and under circumstances of "justifiable homicide."

The following account describes the prevailing behavior of grizzlies at their first meetings with Western Man and also the dangers of provoking "desperate encounters" by taking unnecessary chances. Wootton's attitude toward the grizzly is instructive as it bodes eventual ill for the animal: "the proper thing to do when you see a bear is to kill it." There is no hint of a conservation ethic—no remorse that bears have declined in numbers—no desire to preserve those remaining. Bears were regarded as formidable competitors but of no real value. Respect alone would do little for either the grizzly or the frontiersmen, both of whom would soon be displaced by those bent on "settling" the West. �֍

There was one native of the Rocky Mountain region, which the hunters and trappers always made a point of dealing with very cautiously and circumspectly, and that was the grizzly bear. The grizzly, cinnamon, and black bears were all natives of this region, but the "grizzly" was the "big chief" of the bear family. There used to be a great many of them in the mountains, but we rarely hear of one now. They have a strong aversion to civilization, and have gotten as far away from the settlements as they could get.

I have had a long and intimate acquaintance with the "grizzly," and what I tell you about him may correct some erroneous notions which are prevalent as to the kind of animal he is.

In the first place, let me tell you that he is not a professional man-killer, and never goes about "seeking whom he may devour," as some writers of bear stories would make us believe. That he has been guilty now and then of staining his "chops" with human gore is true, but it was usually under circumstances which would have made "justifiable homicide" a proper verdict, if the affair had been between man and man. It was where he met an open enemy in fair fight, and got the best of it.

My experience has been that the bear will always sacrifice his reputation for courage, to avoid a conflict with the hunter, provided the hunter makes no hostile demonstration, when they come in contact with each other.

An experience which I had one time, just about forty years ago, when hunting in the Cimarron Mountains, will illustrate to what extent the bear is a peace-loving animal.

Early one morning I left my two companions in camp, and started out to get some bear meat. I had not gone more than a hundred yards when I struck the trail of a "grizzly," and after following it about a hundred yards further, through a thick growth of shrub oak, which was about as high as my head, I stepped into a little open space and found my bear. I found him in company with four other bears, all full grown.

I was looking for bear, but I hadn't been appointed a delegate to a convention of "grizzlies," and I felt at once as though I was an intruder. If I had not attracted their attention, I should have retired without making my presence known, or interrupting their deliberations, but they had seen me as soon as I saw them.

I knew that to open hostilities would be suicidal, because, while I might have killed one or two of the bears, I should have been torn to pieces before the row was over if it had once commenced. It was unsafe to retreat, because a bear has no respect for a cowardly enemy, and so I concluded to stand still and give the "grizzlies" to understand that I didn't propose to commence a fuss.

They eyed me closely for about half a minute, and then commenced growling savagely, first taking a few steps toward me and then walking back to where they started from, as though they were daring me to make any hostile demonstration or even to "come half way."

I didn't much like being bullied in that way, but I didn't allow my temper to get the better of my judgement. I stood perfectly still for about five minutes, when the bears seemed to reach the conclusion that they had no quarrel with me, and bringing the proceedings of their convention to an abrupt close, they started off on a run in different directions.

I let them go without firing a shot. Their conduct had been much more genteel than I had expected it to be, and I wasn't going to break the peace under the circumstances.

I think they were even more pleased at getting away from me than I was at getting rid of them. One of them at least must have been panic stricken, because he galloped away toward our camp, and when he reached it, was so much excited that he ran through the camp fire, scattering the sparks all over one of my companions, who happened to be roasting a piece of venison at the time.

There is one thing which a "grizzly" resents very promptly and emphatically, and that is being shot at or threatened with a gun. He understands as well as anybody, that the gun is a death-dealing weapon, and the snapping of the cap, or the click of the hammer, enrages him almost if not quite as much as being wounded. Under such circumstances he fights viciously and ferociously, without any further provocation.

One of the most desperate encounters I ever had personal knowledge of, between the trappers and a "grizzly," was one in which "Dick" Owens, who afterward became somewhat noted as a guide and scout, and John Burris, who, when I last saw him, was a California ranchman, were the participants.

They were out hunting one day and came on to an enormous "grizzly" very unexpectedly. Both the hunters shot at him and both missed. Before the smoke of their rifles cleared away, the bear charged on them, and they made for a small bushy cedar tree, hardly more than a shrub, which was the only tree in sight. Owens was ahead and got into the tree, but Burris had hardly gotten off the ground, when the bear caught him by one foot and dragged him back. He was a man of rare presence of mind, however, and as soon as the bear caught hold of him, he dropped to the ground, and notwithstanding the fact that his body was being scratched and torn in a score of places, he lay perfectly still.

The enraged bear, thinking he had disposed of one of his enemies, left Burris and climbed into the bush after Owens, who had thrown away his gun and could do nothing but engage in a hand to hand fight with old bruin. He struck at the bear with his hunting knife, but the brute caught him by the hand, and then a terrific struggle commenced in the branches of the tree, ten or twelve feet from the ground. Burris, although he was badly wounded, had by this time gotten hold of and reloaded his gun, but it was some little time, an age it seemed to Owens, before he could get in a position to shoot at the bear, without taking great chances on killing his companion, who was having a wrestling match with the animal in the tree top.

Finally he managed to send a bullet through the bear's body, and the big brute dropped to the ground, almost tearing Owens' hand off before loosening its hold.

This shot was not fatal, but the bear left the two hunters and charged down through our camp, which was not far distant from the scene of the encounter. Several more shots were fired at him, and we finally killed him, but both Owens and Burris were left badly crippled, and never entirely recovered.

The hunter who took any unnecessary chances in dealing with a "grizzly," always regretted it. He always discovered that to trifle with the "monarch of the mountains" under any circumstances, was a mistake. Old "Jim" Baker, who next to "Kit" Carson was General Fremont's most noted scout, and who has been my companion on many a trapping expedition, used to tell me how he learned this lesson very early in his experience as a mountaineer, and he would always wind up by remarking, "I haint forgot that lesson yet." Baker came to the mountains about the same time I did, and soon became known as one of the most daring fellows among the mountain men. Two or three years after he came to the country, he and a companion ran across a couple of young "grizzlies" one morning, when they only happened to have with them the butcher knives sticking in their belts. It was not more than a hundred yards to the camp where their guns had been left, but, as Baker said afterwards, "I lowed we could get away with the varmints with our knives, and we sailed into the fight." Baker had a hard tussle with the bear which he attacked, but finally managed to kill him. Just about the time this contest ended, he noticed that his companion had abandoned the fight, and the second bear charged him without stopping to give him a breathing spell, or waiting for time to be called. The struggle which followed between the exhausted hunter and his second antagonist was a desperate one, and poor Baker was more dead than alive, when he again found himself a victor. He could barely drag himself away from the two ferocious animals that he had slain in close combat, and he never again allowed himself to be inveigled into a rough and tumble fight with a "grizzly."

The closest call I ever had myself when hunting bear, was not many years ago, and right here in the Raton Mountains.

Bears were beginning to get scarce in the country then, and I hadn't seen one for a long time. I had boys growing up, and a good many men about me, who were doing different kinds of work, and every now and then some of them would come in and report that they had seen a bear.

I always laughed at them and teased them more or less about their reports, because I thought if there had been any bear in the neighborhood, I should have caught a glimpse of one sometime myself.

One morning I walked out with my gun on my shoulder, thinking I might see something to shoot at, and had not gone more than three or four hundred yards from my house when I came on to an old bear with two good-sized cubs. I thought to myself, "well, the boys were right, after all, and now I'll just teach them that the proper thing to do when you see a bear is to kill it." I calculated to kill the old bear and then capture the two cubs to raise as pets, just to show the travelers through the country what a live Rocky Mountain bear looked like. As I didn't often miss anything I shot at, I had every confidence in my ability to kill the bear at the first shot. For once, however, my confidence in the old rifle, which had served me so many turns, was misplaced. A long period of idleness seemed to have impaired its usefulness. It missed fire, and the snapping of the cap made just noise enough to attract the attention of the bear. I had gotten so close, that when the bear started for me, I could only get out of the way by making for the nearest tree. I reached the tree with the bear in close pursuit, and commenced to climb. It was a small pine tree, and I had grown so stout that I weighed about two hundred and forty pounds, so you can understand that I couldn't climb like a squirrel, even under favorable circumstances. The dry pine limbs that I caught hold of broke under my weight, and when I got about four or five feet from the ground, not high enough to be out of reach of the bear by any means, there I stuck. I couldn't get up, and I needn't tell you that I didn't want to come down. I expected every minute that the bear would take a mouthful of me, but I commenced hunting for a pistol that I had about me, and made up my mind to kill her if she bit a leg off. Just when I thought the biting and clawing was about to commence, something frightened one of the cubs which the old bear had left behind, when she started out to pay her compliments to me, and it set up that peculiar cry, which always makes one think of a child in distress. The old bear left me and ran to the cub, and then they made off together in the bushes. I didn't follow them, because I had seen enough to satisfy me that the bear had an ugly temper.

I really wanted those two cubs, but I didn't want them bad enough to try to get them that morning, at the risk of another encounter with the old lady bear. I let myself down out of the tree, picked up my gun, and walked home. When they asked me what I had found that morning in the way of game, I told them "nothing of consequence." I never said a word about my adventure with the bear, but some way or other the boys found out about it, and for a while I had a hard time to live with them. Every once in a while they would want to know if I had seen any bear lately, and what I thought about there being any in the country.

The thieving propensities of the bear used to get him into trouble with the trappers very frequently. They would come about our camp at night and sometimes carry off meat or sugar, which they found within two feet of a sleeping trapper. If the trapper happened to wake up while the burglary was being perpetrated, the safest thing for him to do was to lie perfectly still and let the burglar have what he wanted, because, like most other burglars, the bear was ready to do some killing if it was necessary to enable him to get away with what he was after.

It takes a good deal of nerve to enable a man to keep quiet when lying in camp at night, with a great ugly brute snuffing about within a few feet of him, but I have done it many a time and never lost my head but once or twice.

Once I was trapping on Indian Creek, a small stream of Southern Colorado, when our camp was visited one night by a "grizzly." A companion named Kincaid slept under the same blanket with me that night, and about the middle of the night, he awakened me out of a sound sleep by giving me a nudge in the ribs. He said something which I thought meant Indians, and pointed toward the foot of our "bunk." Not two yards from our feet I saw a black object which looked to me as tall as a telegraph pole. It was a bear, sitting upon his haunches, as they do sometimes, but I took it to be an Indian, and the next thing I expected was to have a tomahawk hurled at my head. We always slept with our loaded guns at our side, in such a position that we could grab them instantly, and in case of emergency shoot without getting on our feet. Without ever thinking of the thing being a bear, I raised my gun and fired.

As it happened he fell backward over a little bank, and then started off through the brush in an opposite direction from our camp. I had, however, given him his death wound, and he only went a short distance before he fell over a log, and we found him there dead in the morning. If my gun had happened to miss fire, or if I had wounded instead of shooting the bear fatally, I should probably have had as ugly a fight as a man ever had with a mad bear, and I doubt very much whether I should be here now telling stories about my hunting adventures.

I killed another bear under similar circumstances one night, with my hunting knife. I was sleeping soundly when I felt the bear's cold nose rubbed against my face. My hunting knife was in my belt, and when I awakened and found the bear standing alongside of me, I drew the knife and plunged it into his side up to the hilt, springing away from him so quickly that I received but a single scratch. The knife entered his heart and he fell dead on the spot where I had been sleeping a moment before.

To train our horses to carry game, and particularly bear, into camp, was a difficult thing to do. There is nothing on earth that a horse has as greater instinctive fear of than bear, and you can understand how he would feel about having one of the dreaded animals thrown across his back and being compelled to carry it. Even the best broke riding horse would cut more antics than the trick pony at a circus, until he got rid of a load of bear meat, if he had not been put through a previous course of training.

When we wanted to train a horse to carry this kind of a load, the first thing we did was to strip off the skin of a bear, and wrap the green skin about the horse's head. Of course he didn't take kindly to this performance, and made a good bit of fuss about it, but by and by he would quiet down, and then he would carry any kind of a load of game we put on him.

I saw, one time when I was hunting in the mountains along Grand River, a bear which seemed to belong to a different species from those usually seen in this country. I have never seen or heard of any other animal in the mountains that looked like this one, and I have always been at a loss to know what family he belonged to.

I suppose it is hardly possible that a polar bear should be found in this latitude, and yet the animal that I speak of, had every appearance of a polar bear. He was of a dirty white color; would have weighed perhaps five or six hundred pounds, and was certainly the queerest looking bear I have ever seen in these parts.[1] I shot at him and wounded him in the shoulder, but did not succeed in capturing him. It may have been that he was a grizzly, who had turned pale from some cause or other, but if such a thing as finding a polar bear anywhere outside of the region of which he is a native is possible, I shall insist that I have seen one in Colorado, and he wasn't in a cage either.

The bear is the only animal I have found in the Rocky Mountain region, which is at all inclined to attack a man, if there is any way of avoiding a conflict. . . .

[1]Both grizzlies and black bears may vary greatly in color. This is especially so in black bears in the Southwest, where light brown and even blond bears are not uncommon. Jack Wight, a Phoenix taxidermist, once showed me a brownish-gray pelt that was almost slothlike in appearance. Wight said that he had seen a similar animal on only one other occasion.—D. E. B.

A Sporting Adventure in the Far West

John Mortimer Murphy

1860s

No anthology on Southwest bears, especially one featuring grizzlies, would be complete without a California grizzly story. The following episode by John Murphy, a free-lance hunter and writer who traveled extensively throughout the West prior to the advent of railroads and Anglo settlement, is a classic of the times. Published in 1880 by Harper and Brothers of New York under the title *Sporting Adventures in the Far West*, his book attempts to describe accurately all the game animals found west of the Mississippi when only Indians and a few soldiers were present and when the animals were in a more natural state. Hispanic southern California was, of course, the notable exception, having by then been long settled by ranchers and townspeople.

The account, besides being exciting reading, is historically informative, as it documents how the large numbers of grizzlies then present were rapidly eliminated through the use of indiscriminate hunting and poisoning of females and cubs by Mexican sheep ranchers. Murphy lived to rue these depredations on the West's fauna and states in his Preface:

Having no desire to pose as a Nimrod, I may say that some of my hunting was as much for the purpose of studying the *feraenature* as for killing them, and that their life was frequently more pleasing to me than their death. 🌿

One of the pleasantest chases after grizzlies that I enjoyed came off in Southern California. The party, myself excepted, was composed of native Californians and two Mexican Spaniards. As the hunt was organized for the special purpose of driving the bears out of a section of country where they were committing sad havoc among sheep, we selected the best and most experienced mustangs to be found in a large area, and, arming ourselves with rifles and revolvers, we started for the foothills from our rendezvous at 5 P.M., and encamped that night under the shade of some oak-trees, having built a rousing fire to keep away all quadrupedal intruders. After supper we devoted ourselves assiduously up to midnight to puffing cigarettes, singing songs, and relating hunting experiences. The last "story" was told by a swarthy old veteran, and according to that he had killed a bear single-handed with only a hunting-knife, by simply evading a blow of its paw, and then cutting its jugular vein before it could meet his attack. Having slept soundly, we awoke promptly at 4 A.M., and, after partaking of a light breakfast, we loaded our rifles and revolvers, and saddled our steeds, and were in motion in less than an hour.

Deploying in skirmishing order, and in the form of a crescent, we advanced toward a coppice of oaks half a mile in front, which grizzlies were known to frequent. We were accompanied by a dozen mongrel dogs of many breeds, and they were taken by one of the party to the top of a hill, so that they might drive the quarry toward us. He took the precaution to keep to the leeward of the copse, for if even the daring grizzly caught the odor of humanity, it would sometimes think it the better part of valor to beat a rapid retreat. The captain of the skirmish-line gave us orders how to move by the wave of his hand, and all obeyed most promptly. On reaching the wood, we held the reins tighter, grasped the saddle closer with our legs, and placed the barrel of the rifle in the crook of the left arm. This was no sooner done than the dogs gave tongue; the chorus became loud, then broken and general, and in a few minutes after a splendid male grizzly emerged from the bushes, about one hundred yards distant. When he saw the circle around him he hesitated a moment; but the noise of the dogs soon decided his movements, and he made for the opening in front. Bang went a rifle, followed in a second by another. My horse, which had been restless, now showed undoubted terror; he wheeled, and was making for the rear at his best pace; but when I got the reins out of my mouth and into my hands, I gave the Spanish bit a touch that nearly threw him on his haunches, and, wheeling him, I made for my place in the crescent. I found my mustang was not alone in his fright, for I saw two more making their best strides for home. When I reached my position, Bruin was making for that direction, as it was the only opening left. I fired at him twice in rapid succession; but at this moment my mustang became alarmed again at the object approaching, and wheeled to the rear. He had not gone far ere I checked him; caused him to make a demi-volt, and got another shot. Bullets were whizzing thickly around his bearship at this time, and he did not go five yards farther ere he fell, groaning, to the ground, and bleeding profusely. Two revolver-shots in the head finished him, and our prize lay outstretched before us in all his inanimate majesty. Who killed him? Every one was willing to bet or swear that he had hit him, yet, on examining the body, only three bullets were found, though fifty must have been fired. The whole time occupied by this contest did not exceed ten minutes, yet it would seem as though a small army was firing, so rapidly were the leaden missiles poured forth.

After the death the assembly was sounded by a loud halloo, and the runaways returned, swearing, as only Spaniards can, at their ill-luck and their cowardly steeds. Having dragged the bear into some bushes, we reformed our line, and moved in an oblique direction to the right, where the manzanita grew thickly. The dogs had scarcely entered the shrubbery ere a simultaneous yelp made us all halt, and in a few moments a female broke cover; but seeing the number of enemies surrounding her, she re-entered the bushes and made for a ravine on the right. Her course was marked by the swaying of the shrubbery, so to the right we all started at the best speed of our horses, intending to head her off. We had scarcely proceeded half a mile ere we struck a canyon, and into this we had the chagrin of seeing our game hurl herself, for she apparently went to the bottom at one stride. That she was not injured, however, was proved by the yelping of the dogs, which pursued her for over a mile; but I may add that they took very good care not to go too near her.

As we could not do much in the heat of the day, we concluded to return to camp and await the morrow for the resumption of our sport. During the evening, while lying around the fire, everybody was telling just how he missed or hit the bear; but who hit him is to this day a mystery, for the greater number insisted that their bullets struck just where the holes were found. Whoever reached the vicinity of the heart, however, was the champion. The action of our veteran mustangs was accounted for on the ground that Bruin emerged too suddenly, so did not give them time to think. This may have been the cause, but to me it looked like want of courage and experience. Our camp was the scene of hilarity that evening, and the song, "*Hermosa esta la noche*," was sung many times over, and with immense gusto, as all were pleased with the success achieved.

We started out the next morning at six o'clock, and worked up a piece of woods half a mile from the coppice of the previous day, but it proved a blank draw. While we were passing from this to another promising country, we espied a grizzly and her two cubs playing together in a dell in the most affectionate manner; and as we felt sure that they could not escape, we watched their ludicrous and clumsy antics for some moments with keen interest. When weary of that, the dogs and a huntsman were sent to the windward in order to drive the animals to the leeward, where we posted ourselves. As soon as the hounds came in sight of the bears they set up a tremendous yelping, and charged them boldly; but they reckoned without their host, for the entire party stood boldly at bay, and did not make even an effort to avoid their canine foes; and when the dogs came to close quarters the cubs drew near their dam, and all raised themselves on their hind-legs, as if they were willing and ready for the contest.

The dogs tried to get a nip at them, but their effort was in vain, for their ungainly opponents met them in every direction, and frequently charged them in return; but their canine caution and nimbleness enabled them to escape all blows and attempts at a hug. The old grizzly finally became so angry at their pertinacious annoyance that she rushed suddenly at one that approached very close, and, giving him a sweeping blow with her paw, killed him as easily as she would a mouse by crushing his skull. While she was engaged in this affair, half a dozen of the dogs surrounded the cubs and gave them several severe nips, which caused them to howl fearfully, and their cries brought the dam back in a hurry to aid them; but before she could come up, one of the youngsters had killed another of its opponents by breaking his spinal column with a blow, and then biting it through and through. As the entire pack was threatened with destruction if the contest continued, we advanced at a gallop to the scene, and calling the dogs away, though not without much trouble, we opened fire on the old one only, as we wished to lasso the youngsters. When the latter saw the numerous enemies surrounding them they tried to escape into a copse close by, and the mother attempted to follow them; but two or three bullets in her body caused her to stop and face about to deliver battle to her foes. Her eyes fairly gleamed with fury on seeing the men and horses galloping about her; and whenever a cavalier came any way near her she charged him boldly, but only to receive a shot from him or some other person near by. Bullets rained around her from rifle and revolver; but they seemed to have no other effect on her than to rouse her into fury and cause her to charge whenever she had the chance.

A man named Diego Gonzales, becoming incensed at the inefficacy of the fire, or her magical vitality, rode close up to her, as his mustang was well trained, and delivered his fire within ten yards of her face; but he had scarcely discharged his rifle before she bounded toward him; and before he could wheel and get away, she had thrown horse and rider to the ground by one desperate blow. The fallen man drew his revolver, so as to sell his life as dearly as possible; but before he could use it half a dozen men jumped off their terrified mustangs and ran toward her, and, opening fire on the huge beast, they killed her ere she could transfer her attentions from the steed to the rider. When these were examined, we found that the horse was so severely injured that he could not live, while the rider escaped with only a severe contusion of the under side and leg, and the crushing of the ankle-bone. To rid the poor horse of his misery, as his neck and face were horribly cut, he was shot, and Gonzales was taken on a rude litter to camp by four men. The remainder of the party started out after the cubs, and, with the aid of the dogs, we soon found them concealed in a dense growth of manzanita. The party separated on finding them, in order that each might capture one, but, at my request, it was decided not to shoot them there, but to drive them out and capture them alive if possible. When the proposition was agreed to, four of us went after one, and the rest after the other. Driving our cub into open ground, the lariats were soon whirling about its head, and in less than five minutes we had it bound legs and head, so that it could not move either. The other party being equally successful, we placed all our trophies in three wagons and returned to our rendezvous, at the house of Gonzales, as he was too much injured to be able to indulge in any hunts just then, and all wished to show him how much he was respected. I left the neighborhood a few days afterward, but I learned from a correspondent that over twenty grizzlies were killed in that section during the season, though the greater number were poisoned.

A final word might be said about the position of the grizzly in the animal world. Naturalists have called the lion the "king of the beasts," but they evidently knew little of the grizzly at the time they made this decision. If strength and courage are considered as recommendations to royalty in the quadrupedal world, then I think the grizzly ranks above the lion. I have not seen the former perform the feats said to be accomplished by the latter, of trotting away with a heifer in its mouth, as it does not generally carry its prey in that manner, as the *felidae* do; but I have known it to kill an elk weighing five or six hundred pounds, and, in devouring it, to turn it over with the greatest ease. It, so far as my experience and information go, drags its prey along the ground if heavy, but if light it has been known to carry it between its forelegs. In magnanimity of character, if carnivorous animals can possess such a trait, it is equal to the so-called "king of beasts," for it has been known to wound a buffalo severely, then let the poor creature escape. That it has killed two and three buffaloes at a time with strokes of its huge paws is a well-authenticated fact; and it has been, to reiterate, known to drag a heavy bull, that must have weighed from twelve to eighteen hundred pounds, a long distance. I doubt if a lion can do this, and I am rather inclined to think that in a contest between both animals the grizzly would prove the victor. Sportsmen, unless provided with heavy rifles, would therefore do well to beware of it; for there is not a year, I suppose, that some men are not killed by it, owing principally to their own foolhardiness in attacking it with light weapons, or without the aid of companions.

Hunting Bear in the Sangre de Cristos

C. E. *Edwords*

ca. 1883

The following narration from the field notes of L. L. Dyche is from Edwords's *Camp Fires of a Naturalist,* published by D. Appleton and Co. of New York in 1893. Dyche made three expeditions into the Sangre de Cristo Mountains of New Mexico in the early 1880s to collect mammals, birds, and insects for the University of Kansas. In addition to two grizzlies (at least one of which was mounted), Dyche secured black bears, mule deer, a white-tailed deer (a species no longer found in the Sangre de Cristos), and a number of smaller mammals. To his great disappointment, Dyche was unable to collect an elk on these trips and, as a consequence, there are no specimens of New Mexico's native elk in a scientific collection.

In 1895 Dyche was chosen by the U. S. National Museum to head an attempt to rescue Robert E. Peary's exploration party from the Arctic. From 1909, until his death in 1914, Dyche was Kansas State Game Warden, while still remaining attached to the university in Lawrence. Additional biographical details, and the reminiscences of the time his widow spent with Dyche in the Sangre de Cristos, are presented in Elliot Barker's delightful book, *Beatty's Cabin,* published by the University of New Mexico Press in 1953.

Dyche was an experienced naturalist as well as a collector and outdoorsman; his experiences and observations of grizzlies are worth noting. The scientist's rapture on killing the huge grizzly in the following account is obvious. Although he expresses remorse on killing the animal, it is informative to note that neither the scientist nor Edwords say anything about whether, or how, the grizzly should be preserved for posterity as a *living* legend. It is assumed that the bear will disappear even though his great effort to obtain a specimen illustrates the value of the grizzly to Dyche and the scientific community. 🌿

Just at dark on the evening of the third day camp was made [in the Sangre de Cristo Mountains] in a little mountain meadow, and when daylight came next morning, they saw that the place could not have been better chosen. Within seventy-five yards of the tent was a well-worn bear trail, where the brutes had passed from one mountain to the other for years. The place was christened "Camp Bear Trail," and preparations for an extended hunt were made.

There was no doubt that there were plenty of bears in the vicinity, for their trails could be seen all about the place. So confident were Dyche and Brown[1] that they would soon get a bear that they contented themselves with bacon rather than risk scaring away the big game by a shot at a grouse or deer. Every night the burros were brought into camp and tied for fear they would fall a prey to bruin. In a few days the novelty of the situation wore off and Dyche killed a deer, not caring whether the shot scared a bear or not. He went out on the side of the mountain to look for meat, carrying his big Sharp and a number 10 Colt shot-gun so that he would be ready for anything. Hearing a noise in a clump of willows his blood almost boiled with excitement, for from the noise he was sure that a bear was coming. Suddenly the bushes parted and a big mule deer buck trotted out into the opening with head up and ready to jump at the slightest sound. He was on the steep hillside fifty yards above Dyche, who sent a load of buckshot into him and the animal rolled down to within thirty feet of his slayer.

Bear-trails were followed day after day without ever seeing or

[1]Dyche's hired assistant.—Eds.

hearing anything of the animals. An ambush was laid for a deer which came to the little lake every evening for water. While lying in wait, a band of the animals came down to the water's edge to drink. When they were well bunched and not over seventy-five yards away, Dyche discharged "Old Reliable," and as the frightened deer ran he fired three more shots after them. When the smoke cleared away he found that he had done that which no true hunter feels proud of. He had allowed his excitement to get the better of his judgement, and there, as the result of his four shots, lay six fine deer. Four had seemingly been shot through at the first fire. Dyche was ashamed and almost vowed to give up hunting on account of the unwarranted slaughter. He made all the amends in his power, and every pound of meat and all the skins were saved. Brown went down the trail to Harvey's with the meat. In his whole hunting experience thereafter this served as a good lesson. He never again shot at random into a bunch of animals, but always singled out the one wanted for meat or a specimen.

The first night after Brown went down with the meat a big bear passed along the trail, leaving a track as big as a peck measure. Dyche resolved to see where that bear went if it took all summer. With a light lunch in his pocket, a thin rubber blanket, some matches, a hatchet, his rifle, and seventeen cartridges he started on the campaign. The trail was fresh and the bear did not seem to know that he was followed. He went swinging along, leaving a trail that could be followed on the run. Here he had turned over a log and there he had scratched up the earth looking for roots and tender shoots. He wandered around in an apparently aimless manner, and Dyche followed every track. Night settled down and Dyche was at last compelled to give up the chase. He had travelled fully fifteen miles over the mountains and through the forest, and was so tired that he did not think of returning to camp, but finding a sheltered place on a large projecting rock, he spread his gossamer blanket as a wind-break, and on a bed of spruce and fir boughs, with a blazing fire at his feet, he tried to sleep. He was tired, but sleep would not come. He would fall into a doze and build up the fire until morning came. At early dawn he started back to the home camp, and the day was spent resting.

Awaking from a refreshing sleep next morning, Dyche saw where a bear had come over the trail, and, to show his contempt for the hunters, had wallowed in the spring from which they got their drinking-water. Brown returned with mail and provisions from Harvey's and a council of war was held. It was decided to make an ambush and wait until the bear again went over the trail and then kill him. He evidently passed along in the night, and a platform was built in a tree near the trail.

Darkness found Dyche safely ensconced on the platform, prepared for an all-night's siege. A heavy overcoat was supplemented by a blanket and a trunk-strap secured him to the tree in case he should fall asleep. The rifle and shot-gun were within easy reach, and it would have been a bad night for a bear had one come across the trail. All night long, shivering and longing for daylight, Dyche sat there, but never a sound of bear was heard. The stillness was horrible. Not an owl hooted and not a twig was snapped by fox or wolf. The twittering of the early birds at last announced the approach of day, and Dyche crawled down, cold and benumbed, and made his way to camp, where a hot breakfast soon reinvigourated him. Again and still again was this ambush laid. A band of deer went over the trail, and then a fox came and smelled the bait but did not touch it, and a wildcat came along and clawed around, but went on without going near the bait. Dyche let them all go, as he did not want to shoot and run the risk of scaring away a bear. But no bear came. Soon after sunrise on the third morning Dyche crawled into camp for a little breakfast and then hastened back. The bear had been there during his absence. The old fellow evidently came along a few seconds after Dyche left, for he had eaten the whole of the bait which had been left near the trail, and then had scratched up the earth near by. To finish the performance he had wallowed in the little stream and passed on over the mountain.

Dyche was tired, sleepy, sore, and stiff, but this was too much for human endurance and he promptly started on the broad trail left by the animal. The bear went along, turning over logs, stones, and stumps, looking for bugs. Here he wallowed in a mud-hole to relieve himself from fleas, and there he scratched up the earth or stretched himself up on a tree. Dyche could not catch up with him, and at two o'clock in the afternoon he returned to camp almost worn out. A big buck jumped from cover, but he let the animal go. A light supper, and blank until dawn. A hot breakfast restored him and after a whole day spent about the camp he felt like going on another campaign. A fox and a wildcat were caught in traps and the skins taken care of, and then Dyche started out to look at some traps, expecting to be gone about an hour. It was late in the afternoon when he returned, and from the flush in his face and his general excitement Brown knew that he had seen bears. Dyche had had a most wonderful adventure, and was so wild over it that he could hardly wait until after supper to tell his story.

"I got to the fox-traps, and as I was looking around I saw a large bear-trail that was very fresh. The bears had been here, there, and everywhere. The ground was dug up as if a drove of hogs had been rooting and overturning the logs and stones. There must have been a herd of them, for paths led through the woods in a dozen different directions. I took a large circuit in order to find which way they had gone. I soon found the main trail, which was as easily followed as if a herd of cattle had been along there. It went through a number of grassy parks, down a small stream, up another, and then over a mountain. I followed as rapidly as possible, expecting every minute to see them. They spread destruction in their path. Logs, stumps, and stones were turned over and ant-hills torn to pieces. A choke-cherry patch was stripped of berries and leaves. The bushes were torn and stripped and the tops chewed off, presenting a sorrowful sight. I determined to get back to camp and start to-morrow with five days' rations in my haversack, and find those bears or die in the attempt.

"I wandered along revolving my plans in my mind, and came out of the big woods on a mesa about two hundred yards wide, flanked on one side by a heavy forest, while on the other was a sheer fall of several hundred feet. It was a beautiful place, and I thought it would be an amusing occupation to roll stones down the canyon, but was too tired to put the idea into practice. I was walking slowly along, looking now and then towards the woods, but not thinking of seeing anything, when suddenly there appeared at the edge of the timber a number of moving objects. I could not make out what they were, but as there was such a number of them I concluded they must be goats. Mexicans sometimes bring goats up the Pecos River into this country, and I thought a herd might have been driven out of the regular trail. As they appeared to be coming towards me I waited and soon got another glimpse of them about three hundred yards away. They were among the trees, and the sun through the leaves gave them a spotted appearance which convinced me that they were goats, for many of the Mexican goats are spotted. I could not see the herder and stood perfectly still waiting for them to get nearer. Suddenly there came out of the forest, directly to the west of me and not over seventy yards away, a huge grizzly bear.

"Before I could realize what had happened, out came another, then a third, a fourth, a fifth, a sixth, and a seventh. Just think of it, seven big bears in sight all at once! I think there were four more which I saw, making eleven in all in that band. I knew I was in a most desperate situation. On one hand was a bottomless precipice and on the other a herd of the most ferocious animals which range the mountains. How the sweat did roll off of my face! There was only one thing to do, and I did it to perfection. That was to stand perfectly still and let those bears go about their business. I was hunting bears, but not these particular bears. There I stood in perfectly plain view of those animals, but they did not see me. They were walking fast, and I had a splendid opportunity to observe their mode of travel as they passed on.

"I no longer wondered at my not being able to overtake them on the trail. They went swinging along in a sort of shambling trot or canter almost as fast as the gait of a horse. Some would stop for a second at a time, turning over logs and stones, and then hurry on to overtake the band, which moved right along.

"As soon as they were out of sight in the woods to the southwest of me, I hastened to assure myself that I was still alive and wiped the sweat from my face. I could easily have put a bullet through any of them, but what would have happened then? I might have been set upon by the whole gang and would not have made a fair meal for one of them. I made haste to get into the woods and tried to head them off. I wanted to get a shot at them where I could get shelter in the trees if they attacked me. They unintentionally outwitted me, how-ever, and went up a ridge while I was watching a stream."

"Well, I have a scheme," said Brown. "Let me go back to Harvey's and then down to Las Vegas and get a big bear-trap, and we will get a bear, sure. It will take some time, but it seems that we are spending more time than anything else, anyway."

"Well, as we need more provisions I guess you'd better make the trip to-morrow," was the reply, and so it was settled. Brown got an early start next morning and Dyche was left alone. The trip would take about ten days to go and return. Dyche started for the woods to see if he could get another look at this bear herd.

On the evening of the ninth day after Brown left, Dyche heard the song of a burro down the canyon and he hastened to get a warm supper for Brown, who he knew was coming. From the back of old Reuben dangled a fifty-pound bear-trap. Hot coffee, biscuits, and broiled steak were soon smoking on the table, and Brown went ravenously to work on them.

"This venison is mighty tough," he remarked, "It must have been one of the oldest bucks in the mountains."

"Take another piece," said Dyche.

"It will be better after we've had it a week or two," was Brown's comment, as he took an extra tough bite. "What kind of meat is this, anyhow? It's the toughest venison I ever tasted."

"Maybe it's fox."

"Fox nothing. It's more like burro-meat, I should say. I didn't leave any of the jack here when I went away, did I?"

Dyche could keep his story no longer and burst out with: "It's bear-meat, man. A regular old grizzly at that."

"What? got a bear! Well, if this is a piece of him it must have been the one old Noah had in the ark. Well, I'm glad he didn't get you. Where's the skin? How did you get him?"

"The day you left camp I started out to look at that big trail where my herd went along. I thought there might be some satisfaction in looking at the track if I couldn't see the bears. The trail was a day old, but I followed along without exactly knowing why. After following it for miles I started back to camp, and reached a grassy slope on the side of the mountain and sat down to rest in the edge of it. There was a willow patch in front, and to the east of me and across from the willows was an almost impenetrable forest of spruce trees. Flowing through an opening in this forest was a little stream which joined another rivulet flowing from the willows. As I sat on a log looking across this stream at the spruce forest I saw something moving among the trees, and from the glimpse I got of it among the spruce branches I thought it was a deer. I watched very carefully, expecting to see a big mule buck step out into the opening.

"To my great astonishment a huge grizzly bear stepped from the forest at the opening made by the little stream. What a monster he was! He must have been as big as a cow. The wind was in his favour, and getting scent of me he placed his front feet on a log and began sniffing the air. I could see his big head going up and down, and must confess that I felt a little chill run over me. The old Sharp's rifle always seemed so big and heavy before, but now I wished it was a cannon. I took the best aim possible, holding my breath to prevent muscular movement, and remembering the advice of my father to always see that the sights were on the gun before pulling the trigger, then I fired. The gun belched forth its load with a roar which was echoed by another roar from the bear.

"Here he came growling, rolling, tumbling, falling, jumping, and bellowing, making a terrific noise. I slipped off my shoes, reloaded the gun, placed a handful of cartridges in the crown of my hat by my side, and waited. I thought the whole gang might appear and wanted to be ready for any emergency. The old fellow came on towards me, and I determined that if he ever crossed that stream I would give him another 520-grain bullet. He would get tangled up in a fallen spruce tree and would tear himself loose in a most wonderful manner. Now he was in the willows, rolling and tumbling and biting everything that was in his way.

"His strength and activity were simply wonderful. One blow of his mighty paw would have killed the greatest prize-fighter that ever lived. I have heard stories of men killing grizzly bears with their knives, but I don't think it possible for twenty men to have stood before that bear in his death-agony. I could now see him very plainly, and could see that he was covered with blood and was getting weaker and weaker every minute as he came on towards me. Just as he reached the edge of the water he spread himself out on all-fours, and there continued throwing up his head, uttering most horrible groans and guttural grunts, while I sat cold and spell-bound under the great excitement. At last he died, seventeen minutes after he had received a ball which would have been instant death to an ox. Then I got up and went over to where he lay.

"He was a monster indeed. Not fat but so muscular. Streams of blood were running from his mouth where he had broken his great teeth in his death-agony. I was under intense excitement, but I noticed that his legs were black while his sides and back were of a tawny tint. His tail was very short, so short, in fact, that he could not even sit down upon it.

"It had been raining all day, but I never noticed it as I sat on the log watching the dying throes of the bear. I must confess that I had a pang of remorse as I looked down at the dead monster. I had at last outwitted one of the giants of the forest, but in his death I had seen the qualities of a grand warrior. After finishing my examination of the big fellow I turned about and went to camp, leaving him just where he had fallen. I reached the camp at dark, and would have given a good deal if you had been here to share the enthusiasm with me.

"There was no sleep for me that night. I went over that fearful struggle again and again, and when I dozed off I would wake with a start from a frightful dream of the bear. Next morning I was rested but not refreshed, and after a hurried breakfast I hastened down the canyon where I had left the dead bear. It seemed at times as if it might all be a dream—but no, when I got to the spot there he lay, just as I had left him the night before, dead and cold. Having spent about two hours in taking seventy measurements for future reference, I skinned him. I found that the old fellow had been shot before, for there were two bullets about the size of a forty-four Winchester imbedded in his body, one in his hip and the other in the shoulder. My ball hit him fairly in the neck, cutting the jugular vein and passed entirely through the body, coming out about six inches from the tail near the spine.

"I was almost worn out, but I carried the meat, skin, and head to the big snow-drift and buried them, and dragged myself to camp, where I ate a light supper and then rolled up in my blankets and slept until dawn next morning."

During the succeeding days Dyche thoroughly dressed the skin. All fat and flesh were removed and the feet skinned down to the very toe-nails, and all ligaments removed from the bones. A preparation of one part alum and four parts salt was now rubbed all over the skin. The feet and head were folded in and then saturated with a strong solution of the mixture. This operation was repeated in twenty-four hours and then again in twenty-four, and the skin was ready to be hung up to dry.

Susie—Queen of the "Spoilt" Grizzlies

Montague Stevens

1883

Montague Stevens, a one-armed Englishman, owned and operated the vast S. U. Ranch, headquartered at Horse Springs in what is now Catron County, New Mexico. A gentleman-rancher, educated at Cambridge, Stevens had friends in high places in the U. S. Army and was personally acquainted with President Theodore Roosevelt. He often guided notable sportsmen on big-game hunts in his ranchlands, and himself became enamored with the sport of bear hunting. Between 1889 and about 1905, he devoted much of his energy to raising bear hunting dogs and became fascinated with the ways of the grizzly. These he hunted in the Datil and San Mateo mountains, as well as the mountains of Catron County.

The knowledge gained from these hunts, and the adventures experienced along the way, are well described in his only book *Meet Mr. Grizzly*, published by the University of New Mexico Press in 1943 and recently reprinted by High-Lonesome Books, Black Range Station, San Lorenzo, New Mexico. The story of "Susie—Queen of the 'Spoilt' Grizzlies"[1] appears toward the end of the book and takes

---

[1] A "spoilt" or "spoiled" grizzly was one that had previously been trapped or brought to bay by hounds and escaped. Once educated, such a grizzly was *spoilt* and difficult to capture again.

place after Stevens's grizzly-hunting techniques had been refined and he had attained a reputation as an accomplished bear hunter.

The story, besides being an exciting account, also communicates Stevens's attitude of respect and honor for the grizzly. Indeed, Stevens thought the extinction of the grizzly would be a great tragedy and, unlike most of his contemporaries, he later spent some time and effort to preserve the species. 🐾

Only a few days previous, a ranchman, whose range ran along the west side of Crosby Mountain in the Datil Range, sent me word that a grizzly had been killing his cattle, and to bring my hounds and try to catch this bear. I moved my camp over to Crosby Mountain, then went over and visited the ranchman, who told me that the bear had killed a cow at the Crosby Springs a couple of days before, and was supposedly still eating on it. This was most welcome news to me. He went on to say that this grizzly was known as "Susie," sometimes "Big Susie," because she was a very large bear, and was known to have run on Crosby Mountain for a great many years.

It was then that I realized that this was the same bear that Dan and I had run three years before, when Miss Agnes Morley (Mrs. Cleaveland) was with us, an episode which is so well described in her *No Life for a Lady*. I well remember that hunt, and Susie winning the round by getting away from us.

It happened that Dan and I were camping at the Morley Ranch, and we had been told that this grizzly and two cubs were "using" on Crosby Mountain. By a great piece of luck, it had snowed a little during the night, and early next morning, Dan and I started out on our hunt, joined by Miss Morley. As the snow had obliterated all old tracks, any that we might run onto would not be more than a few hours old. On the north hillside, where the sun did not strike, the old snow was still deep.

In the afternoon, we struck the trail of Susie and her cubs. The ground was still thinly covered by snow, and we could easily follow by sight, while as it was thawing, the hounds had no difficulty in trailing. They soon got out of hearing, but this, for once, made no difference, since the bear tracks in the snow were easy to follow. After running some ten miles, we heard the hounds baying at some place where the bear must have stopped, and which turned out to be a cave, probably the one Susie had picked out in which to hibernate with her cubs.

The cave was on a steep north hillside, and had been dug out under a flat ledge of rock that skirted the hill. A big, dead pine had fallen up hill, the roots sticking up in the air about ten feet below the cave. The hounds were baying furiously in the space that lay between the cave and the roots of the tree. We approached a spot about fifty feet above the cave, and dismounted, tied up our horses and held a council of war.

I knew that Miss Morley was very anxious to kill a grizzly, a feat that no other girl had ever accomplished, so far as we knew. Our problem was to figure out a way in which she could do this without any risk. Miss Morley suggested that we should all go down to the cave together, but I remembered the responsibility I had assumed when I promised her mother that I would look out for her safety. Under such circumstances, it seemed to me preferable to face a wounded grizzly rather than an irate mother whose daughter had gotten hurt in spite of my promise that she would come to no harm. So Miss Morley's suggestion was politely declined.

About thirty feet from the cave, and facing it, stood a young pine, and one of its sturdy branches, some ten feet from the ground, was a suitable place for a person to sit and shoot at the bear. So we decided that Miss Morley should climb the tree and await developments. Dan loaned her his rifle, keeping his six-shooter as his only weapon, and then climbed another tree close by.

While the vantage points of Miss Morley and Dan were strategically correct, as was also the bear's in the cave, I realized that the continuation of such a procedure would be very inconclusive; that is, it would only lead to a bear-hunting stalemate. In order to avoid such a contingency, I thought it was best to go to the cave and investigate.

Stooping low, I approached the fallen tree at a point facing the mouth of the cave. I then pushed my rifle onto the trunk of the tree, and raised my head slowly, to look over. Unfortunately, the cave was between me and the setting sun, whose rays shone directly into my eyes, and I was obliged to pull my hat down and peer into the cave from under the brim.

For the first few seconds I could see nothing. Then, in the semi-darkness of the cave, I saw the outline of Susie's head and her glinting, beady eyes, looking straight at me. I moved my rifle slowly to aim, and I needed only one more second for a perfect shot. But Susie didn't grant me that second. She bolted out of the cave straight at me—as Dan subsequently expressed it: "Like a bat out of Hell"—and as I moved the sun's rays blinded me, and all I could do was to thrust my rifle forward in the hope that it would go down her throat.

Unluckily, I missed my aim, and the rifle went off, kicking itself out of my hand onto the ground, side-swiping her neck, and inflicting only a slight flesh wound.

I bent over to pick up the rifle, but at that moment, Susie appeared around the roots of the tree, and took after me. I ran up alongside the tree trunk, and realizing she was gaining on me, took a cartwheel header over the log into the snow on the other side, and rolled onto the ledge of rock which was just above the cave.

At the same instant, Miss Morley fired, and Dan, thinking that she had hit me, shouted, "You've killed him! You've killed him!"

These remarks were hardly calculated to induce her to act in a normal way, especially as Dan kept yelling repeatedly, "Kill the bear! Kill the bear!"

Though, perhaps I should say that, in his excitement, he didn't express himself in exactly those polite terms. It is not surprising, therefore, that Miss Morley should have continued snapping her rifle at the bear without putting in a fresh cartridge.

Meanwhile, I picked myself up and pulled out my six-shooter, while the two cubs came running out of the cave to where I was, and, standing up, one on each side of me, their heads being even with my shoulders, grunted like scared hogs.

All this time, Susie was milling round under Miss Morley's tree, while the dogs kept baying at her furiously. The cubs and I were looking anxiously at the tree trunk, expecting Susie to come over it, but with entirely different emotions. The cubs were looking forward to a family reunion, which I certainly was not.

It was one of those moments when you have to think quickly, and I concluded to vacate the conspicuously undesirable spot on which circumstance had placed me by jumping down off the ledge and running into the cave, leaving it up to Susie, in her turn, to get *me* out. Fortunately, I was not called upon to take this course as the baying of the hounds began to recede, indicating that Susie had decided to retire from the field of battle.

As soon as the full import of this dawned on me, I plucked up courage and shoved my six-shooter into the ribs of one of the cubs and fired. He fell forward into the snow, kicking, but the other one disappeared before I could treat him the same way. I then ran around the roots of the tree to where my rifle lay and, picking it up, climbed the hill to where I had tied my horse. Scrambling onto his back, I pulled out after Dan, who had already started off after the hounds and Susie, whose trail was marked with occasional drops of blood on the snow.

We had not pursued her very far until it became dark, so we called the dogs to follow us, and returned to camp the way we had come, passing the cave, but we found that Miss Morley had already left.

And now the time had at last come when I was to hunt Susie for the second time. Having been told exactly where I would find the cow that Susie had killed at Crosby Springs, I started out the next morning to hunt her. I headed straight for the dead cow, with all the dogs, including Sleuth, following close at my horse's heels. When I got within about fifty yards of the cow, I dismounted, leaving all the dogs, except Sleuth, to stay with my horse. Sleuth ran ahead of me, and at once scented a bear trail and started after the pack.

From the lively way the hounds bayed, I knew it was a hot trail, and it was not long before they got out of hearing. After some five miles, with my slow-trail dogs pointing the way, I again got in hearing of the hounds, but this time the baying remained in the same place, from which I knew the bear was either bayed, or up a tree. Listening on, I noticed that the hounds were barking alternately, which meant that they had treed a black bear. If they had been baying Susie, a grizzly, she would have made an occasional run at them, which would have caused them to bark simultaneously, with a sort of scared bark.

This was an unexpected blow to me, as I had felt sure that the hounds were running Susie. But there was nothing I could do about it, except to ride to the tree and shoot the bear out of it.

After the dogs had had their customary meal, I rode back to camp and sent Telesfor out with a pack horse to bring it in.

The reason for the hounds taking the black bear's trail, instead of Susie's, was because it was the hotter of the two. Susie had come in first, and had eaten on her kill, and after she had left, the black bear came along and took his turn at eating, thus leaving the stronger and later scent.

Ordinarily, the catching of this black bear would have no special significance, but in this case it was different, for I was much worried over the fact that Susie might have heard the hounds baying this bear, in which case it might have resulted in her leaving Crosby Mountain, like any ordinary "spoilt" bear would have done. I presume the reason she didn't was that as she had been run by hounds before and, having gotten away successfully, she must have developed a certain contempt for them. She would have gotten away this time, had it not been for my double-header trailing stunt, one that she could never have figured on.

Early next day, I started out and, like the day before, as soon as Sleuth reached the cow, he started off on a hot trail, which this time really was Susie's, although at first I was afraid that it might be that of another black bear.

The hounds soon got out of hearing. For the first few miles the going was good, until I reached a deep canyon, the side of which was too steep for a horse to go down. I decided to go to the left to find a place where I could cross, which was the wrong choice.

Panther and Wolf had already started down into the canyon, so I had to blow my whistle to call them back to me. With these dogs ahead of me, side by side, I rode down about a mile before I could find a place to cross the canyon. I went up on the other side, and when I reached a point that was opposite to where the bear and pack had gone down into the canyon, Panther and Wolf continued on, show-ing that the bear and pack must have changed their direction. I went on for another mile before I could again drop into the canyon, and then I went down it with the expectation of striking the trail at any moment. I had gone but a quarter of a mile when, on passing the mouth of a side canyon, Panther and Wolf suddenly took up it, and sure enough, on its sandy bed were Susie's tracks, with hound tracks occasionally showing up in them, proving positively that we were on Susie's trail, and not that of another bear.

We followed the trail up this side canyon until it headed up on the mountain, through the usual thick timber and quaking aspen thick-ets, which grew profusely around the northern end of the mountain top. There were, however, places where the timber was not so thick but what I could ride through it. So calling Panther and Wolf off the trail to join me, as I could no longer follow the dogs, it was through one of these gaps that I rode to the top of the mountain.

All this time I was out of earshot of the hounds, but I knew the general direction in which they were headed, so I followed along near the edge of the timber until finally I did hear them.

Susie had evidently stopped to rest, because the sound of the baying was stationary. I rode on to a point about five hundred feet above where she had stopped in a quaking aspen thicket. The wind was in her favor; that is, there was no steady wind from any one direction, though had there been one, I could have directed my movements in such a way that she could not have winded me when I tried to approach her.

While this particular day might be called a "still" day, the air was not motionless. Little currents of air would start up from somewhere, and after a brief but erratic existence, end in the same place, confirm-ing the Biblical saying that "The wind bloweth where it listeth." This gave Susie a great advantage, because no matter from what angle I might approach, these tell-tale, fitful gusts of wind would give me away, causing Susie to get a move on.

As she dashed straight away from me, I could only infer that she must have winded me, which was the last thing I wanted her to do. When I left my horse and wormed my way down the mountainside to within about fifty yards of her, she would then suddenly bolt, and every time I decided to follow her, she wouldn't stop long enough for me to get a shot. I would follow her until I got temporarily exhausted, and then I would have to give up and wend my weary way back to my horse, George, who, by this time, was half a mile or more away. Then I would clamber into the saddle and leave it up to him to continue the chase, while I would rest and get back my wind. This was my advantage.

But Susie also had an advantage, aside from the wind. Though contrary to the rules of war, while she was on the defensive, she still held the initiative, and by forcing me to make detours most of the time, I was compelled to travel two or three times as far as she did. But to offset this, George and I could chase her on a sort of double shift basis; that is, when I had to make these quaking aspen excursions on foot, George would have a good rest, and when I would get back in the saddle, it was my turn to take it easy.

It was a sort of game of hide and seek. Hour after hour, all day long, I had chased her from one quaking aspen to another, and it was now mid-afternoon. It began to sink into my brain that if she could wind me every time I came near her, and run away before I could get a shot, keeping up those tactics until dark, she would win this round.

So far, the battle had been even, in that while I had never caught up with her, she had never got away from me. Luckily for me, she took this latter view into consideration, and decided upon some other method of giving me the slip.

Instead of continuing to dodge back and forth between the quaking aspen thickets, she suddenly left them, and ran toward the southern end of the mountain, where there was little timber or brush. I was at least a half mile away from George, and the time it took to get back to him gave her a good start.

I galloped in the direction in which the baying of the hounds showed she had gone, and it was not long before Panther and Wolf again picked up their trail.

The southern end of the mountain was a big, rocky, flat mesa, about nine thousand feet high, around which was a rimrock, or wall of rock, some eight or ten feet high, in which there were a few gaps.

Susie went across this mesa, and going down through a gap on the east side, she ran along the wall to the south side, and then on to the west side to a big gap immediately above a rock slide, which descended abruptly for about a thousand feet. This rock slide was some two hundred feet wide, and was composed mostly of flat, sharp rocks sticking up in all directions, with some roundish rocks of various sizes scattered about here and there.

As I rode over the mesa, I heard the hounds baying after Susie, who was running along the foot of the rock wall, so I made straight for this gap, and got there the same time she did, neither of us seeing the other until we were only about thirty feet apart. She stopped, raised up on her hind legs and looked at me, then whirled round, and bolted down the rock slide. She very soon lost her balance, and went heels over head, but when she caught on her feet again, she was going so fast that she was unable to stop until she reached the bottom. She had loosened a lot of the roundish rocks, and they pursued her all the way down, a few of them hitting her square on the back. This would have caused her to increase her pace, if that had been possible.

Little did I think, as I watched her plunge down, that this rock slide would be the determining factor in giving me the decision in this second, and what proved to be final round with Susie.

The hounds, of course, followed her down the rock slide, stepping very gingerly over the sharp rocks, and they were only about one-third of the way down when Susie reached the bottom.

Meanwhile, I had to dismount and lead George to one edge of the rock slide before we could start down the mountain. The descent was so steep that I had to step aside, from time to time, to let George slide by me when he lost his balance, but as soon as I got to where I could ride, I remounted and followed the hounds, who were by this time a mile away.

I had with me Panther and Wolf, Twist, the three bull terriers, and Princess. Susie was evidently heading for one of the big caves on a rocky peak, known as Sugar Loaf, and if I didn't reach her before she crossed the narrow valley between Crosby Mountain and Sugar Loaf, my chances of getting her that day were very slim indeed.

After galloping some two or three miles, I again heard the hounds baying. I could hardly believe my ears, because the way in which they bayed indicated that Susie had stopped. When I got to within about fifty yards of her, my bull terriers pushed forward to attack her. I jumped off my horse and pulling my rifle from its scabbard, ran to a tree about ten yards from where Susie was bayed, and stood behind it, ready to shoot at the first opportunity. I didn't have to wait long before she came rushing out from under a big juniper tree into a small open space in front of me.

Grip had her by the throat, Biz by the left ear, and Nap by the right ear. At first she tried to shake this weird canine pendant and earrings loose, but that didn't work. Then she turned her head to the left, trying to get hold of Biz; then the other way, to catch Nap. But like apples bobbing out of reach of a boy's mouth, they stayed out of reach of her jaws. After several such vain attempts, she decided to confine her efforts to catching Biz. She turned faster and faster, in order to grab him, but the only result was that the three bull terriers, by centrifugal force, revolved at a tangent. After about three revolutions, Susie concluded that this wouldn't work, so she stopped and sprang into the air and shook herself. But that didn't work, either. So when she struck the ground, she lowered her head, and rubbing the ground with it, she literally scraped the dogs off her ears, flinging Biz to the left and Nap to the right.

Grip, however, was still hanging tenaciously to her throat, her head being just under the bear's lower jaw, which prevented Susie from biting her, so Susie raised up on her hind legs, and with her forepaws tried to push Grip's body into her mouth.

At that moment, Nap, who had got back on his feet, sprang at her to renew his hold on her ear, but quicker than a flash, for I never saw it, Susie struck him in mid-air. He went hurtling through space, body and tail wiggling, as he tried to regain his balance, until he struck the stump of a pine about seven feet up from the ground, and about twenty feet away.

With all his ribs on one side caved in, he fell to the foot of the stump, limp and helpless. Susie then repeated her attempts to bite Grip, but at that moment I shot her through the brain and she dropped dead.

Incidentally there is a general impression that bears hug, not amicably like human beings, but aggressively. What basis there is for this belief I do not know, but as far as my experience goes I have seen numberless bear and dog fights, but have never seen the least tendency on the part of the bear to hug his opponent. On the contrary, when Grip had Susie by the throat, the latter, not being able either to bite or strike her with her paws, raised up her hind feet and tried to push Grip's body which was hanging down over her breast, into her mouth. If a bear's natural instinct was to hug, she would never have passed up such an opportunity as this to have hugged Grip to death.

Grip kept on biting her as though nothing had happened, and then all the dogs piled onto the luckless Susie, "wooling" her, with the exception of Princess, who, remembering her previous experience with a seemingly dead grizzly, took no interest in the proceedings.

When I thought that the dogs had "wooled" Susie enough, I drove them off, and then it was that I discovered why Susie had stopped when she did. Upon looking at her front feet, I found that the pads had been cut to pieces, leaving shreds hanging from the side. Owing to the great momentum forced upon her by the steepness of the rock slide, she was unable to control her pace, and thus prevent the soles of her feet being cut up as they were. The pain must have been so excruciating that it was impossible for her to continue her flight.

Had it not been for this, she would have got into one of the large caves on Sugar Loaf without my having had a chance to get a shot at her; and even if she didn't, with night coming on, it would soon have been too dark to shoot.

I often have been asked how hard a blow a grizzly can strike. While this is a very difficult question, perhaps I can give some idea of how it might be answered.

Poor Nap weighed forty-five pounds, and when Susie struck him, he went through the air for twenty feet, and I am sure he would have gone another twenty feet had he not been stopped by the pine stump. While I do not feel competent to estimate how hard a blow that would represent, it is possible that some astute mathematician might be able to figure it out.

As a further possible estimate for another angle, I would add that once I came across one of my bulls who had been killed by a grizzly. This bull weighed at least twelve hundred pounds, but nevertheless, his huge neck had been broken as easily as that of a cow by a blow with one paw,[2] while in addition, his whole face had been bashed in, evidently by a blow from the other.

The defeat of Susie was the red-letter day of all my hunting experiences. It marked the gratifying culmination of years of hard work and painstaking mental effort, and proved that bloodhounds could be trained to trail any animal successfully, without having had any previous experience in hunting that particular animal.

[2]A supposition by Stevens not borne out by later investigations. Grizzlies do not break the necks of animals by delivering a blow to the head. The "broken necks" noted by livestock operators, while real, were the result of biting and "wooling" the carcasses.—Eds.

A Hunting Adventure

William French

ca. 1885

Captain William John French was a British remittance man who came to New Mexico in 1883 and took up residence at the W. S. Ranch at the invitation of its owner, Mr. Harold C. Wilson of Cheltenham, England. During the next several years French learned the cattle business, eventually becoming manager of the W. S., then located on the San Francisco River in the Keller Valley about a mile from Alma and about 40 miles south of Montague Stevens's S. U. Ranch. Later, after French became a U. S. citizen, he and Wilson became partners in a 130,000-acre ranching enterprise near Springer in Colfax County, New Mexico. French retired a wealthy man.

"A Hunting Adventure" is excerpted from his *Further Recollections of A Western Ranchman*, edited by J. C. Dykes, and published by Argosy-Antiquarian, New York, 1965. This work and its predecessor, *Recollections of A Western Ranchman* (reprinted by the same publisher from the 1927 edition), detail his life on the W. S. near Alma from 1883 until ca. 1899. It is the later volume, made up of material that was edited out of the earlier work, which contains most of the descriptions of wildlife, and it is fortunate that Dykes saw fit to publish French's entire recollections. French was well educated, and he also possessed an accomplished literary style. Consequently, his books are good reading as well as informative and, as far as I can tell, quite factual.

What makes *Recollections* . . . more than interesting and of particular value to the work at hand is that French had the British penchant for natural history inquiry. His books contain several valuable accounts of wildlife in the 1880s. He is one of the very few actually to see "Merriam elk," and he is the first to describe the sport of hunting Mearns' quail. French took a great interest in the grizzlies which inhabited his ranch and kept several as pets. His several accounts of grizzlies are therefore some of the best to be found in Southwest literature. "A Hunting Adventure" is no exception.🦌

The only thing I can remember in connection with Puckett's reign or interregnum was an adventure we had with a bear, when I was trying to initiate him into the mysteries of that very intricate and rough country which lay at the head of the Pueblo and between there and Blue Creek. It resulted in my becoming the possessor of two little cubs, genuine baby bears which afforded us a good deal of entertainment for the short period of their existence.

The mother also, I might observe, entertained us to the best of her ability as long as she was allowed to and but for a lucky chance, which might be described as an accident, might have put an end to the career of my friend Puckett. We were riding through the mountains near the head of the West Fork of the Pueblo, a country consisting of a labyrinth of winding cañons which started out in all directions and generally ended up in exactly the opposite one to that which you supposed they would. They undoubtedly reached the main stream eventually, but I was never able to follow one of them down completely, without climbing out several times to the top of the mountain to get my bearings. A tedious process, but very necessary, especially towards evening, if you didn't want to get lost and spend the night there, or wandering about the mountains in search of camp, till you stumbled into another equally as bad or worse.

Well, this was in daylight and we were just ferreting some of them out, in search of mavericks, as we had run across some tracks and fresh signs of what were presumably wild cattle. We were following an old game trail which wound up the side of the cañon and ran close under the rim-rock and were making our way with difficulty. In fact the going was so bad that we debated the propriety of turning round and returning to camp and letting the mavericks, if there were such, go to Jericho, or elsewhere.

We were about sixty feet or perhaps more from the rim-rock in a direct line, but much further if we kept to the trail, when our attention was attracted by a peculiar noise which appeared to be proceeding from a cavity, that ran under the rim-rock. It was a kind of puling or whining, that might have been made by a kitten or puppy that might have been suddenly disturbed in his sleep, or deprived of sustenance, which he or she was enjoying. It wasn't the least like anything one expected to hear in the mountains, so we resolved to investigate.

We both dismounted and as Puckett had a gun with him and I was unarmed, he took the lead and I followed a few feet behind him, leading the horses. We hadn't proceeded very far in the direction of the cavity when we met with unexpected opposition, a great she-bear. Her sex we discovered afterwards, at the time that question was of no particular interest; but she came out of the hole, or cavity and came very swiftly, snuffing and snorting and evidently very much annoyed and excited at our interruption.

She came straight for Puckett, rolling the rocks and things down the mountain and all about us. I looked to see him raise the gun to his shoulder, but he didn't. He seemed paralyzed for a moment and then began to shoot from his hip, with the muzzle pointing towards her, as if he was doing it mechanically. All this I observed from the shelter I was in behind him, till the horses I was holding began plunging and rearing and attempting to get away and it took me all my time to control them. All the rest of the situation I was able to take in came just in glances from the corner of my vision.

To me the bear appeared to be as large as an elephant or maybe larger; at any rate she seemed about to eat Puckett, or at any rate chew him up and she was almost on top of him and only within a foot or two of his gun, when he appeared to have hit her. At any rate she rolled over and kept on rolling for two or three hundred yards at least, down the steep side of the mountain, till she was brought to a halt close to the bottom against something.

There she lay perfectly still and I supposed he had killed her. Anyway as soon as I could get the horses quiet, I threw him the bridle of his one and mounted my own. He was all shaken up and quite pale from the experience and so I told him that if he would give me the gun, I would ride down to where the bear was and make sure she was done for. This he gladly did and I hurried down the mountain side as fast as I could, or rather as fast as I could persuade my horse to go, in places where it was necessary for him to assume an attitude as if he intended to stand on his head.

I must have got within a hundred yards or so, perhaps a little closer to the animal we supposed to be dead, when it began to move, rolled over on to its feet and began to shuffle away, as if nothing was the matter with it. I jumped off as quickly as I could and getting down on one knee, took deliberate aim at it. I suppose I must have been a bit shaky, for though I seemed to hit it, all the result it had was to make it go faster. I then threw in another cartridge as I supposed, without taking the gun from my shoulder and taking very careful aim this time, so as to make sure, I pulled the trigger and all the result it led to was a dull click of the hammer.

It was evident the gun was not loaded or the cartridge had failed to go into the chamber. It was necessary to investigate, so I removed the gun from my shoulder and found the magazine was empty. It was evident there was only one cartridge in it when Puckett gave it to me, the one in the chamber. Meantime the bear disappeared into the brush at the other side of the cañon and we saw no more of her, at least for that day.

Before going back to join Puckett, I thought I would look over the place the bear was when I shot at her. It seemed to me that I had hit her and she appeared to be limping a bit when I last got sight of her. When I did so, I found some blood, just a spot or two every few yards or so, but whether the result of my shot or the one from Puckett that knocked her over, it was difficult to say. The place where she had been lying, was all tramped up, but I could find no trace of blood there.

It was getting late however, so I concluded I had better join Puckett, who was still where I had left him, only he was sitting down apparently resting himself. We still had to investigate the cavity where the old bear came from and see if she had not, as we surmised, left some cubs there as only very young animals could be guilty of making the noise we heard. When I got back to Puckett he had completely regained his composure and as he could see everything I did since I left him, it was unnecessary to explain my actions. All I regretted was that the magazine was empty and he said it was full with one cartridge in the chamber when he began, so that he must have got off at least five shots before he hit her and we both agreed that his last shot was a lucky one. Had it failed he might have gone back to camp as a bundle, that is if the bear did not get us both.

The babies were still puling and mewing and evidently much disturbed by the sudden departure of their parent, so we left the horses where they were and went up on foot as fast as we could to their rescue. There was no difficulty in locating them, it was evident they were not far in, but the entrance was narrow. Puckett was far too big to get into it, but I managed to squeeze in with some effort. Inside it was roomier and there was some dim light that got in from somewhere, but it was evident the babies were very young and could not see anything, for they stumbled about aimlessly. I seized each of them by a hind leg and proceeded to back out the way I came in, a task not quite so simple, as an abrasion of the epidermis between my shoulders which I late dicovered bore witness. However, with the aid of Puckett who pulled vigorously on my legs, I succeeded. The little beggers were about the size of month-old Newfoundland puppies and their eyes were not open.

It was evident they could only be a few days old and the next question was how to dispose of them or get them to camp and to the ranch where we could take care of them. The difficulty was finally solved by one of us taking off his chaps, or *chapareras*, the leather covering one wore over the legs, to save one's clothes from being torn. We tied up the bottoms of the legs, dropped one in each side and slung them over the saddle in front. There they could squirm all they wanted to and come to no harm. In this way we packed them safely to camp, all the time being fearful least the old bear should come back in search of them.

When we got there all we could offer them in the way of refreshment was to rub grease on their noses and let them lick it off. When night came they snuggled up in the blankets with us and went quietly off to sleep. The next morning I dispatched them to the ranch in the same conveyance in which we had carried them, with instructions to Considine who was there to feed them warm milk and look after them till I got home. My reason for not accompanying them was that Puckett and I had agreed to try and hunt the mother up. We knew she was wounded somewhere and looked forward to having no great difficulty in trailing her up.

As a fact there was no great difficulty for the first few miles. There were frequent splashes of blood, appearing every few yards or so. The trail led up a steep mountain to the top of the divide and then along a fairly open mesa, covered here and there with large patches of live-oak brush. These thickets were dense and impenetrable for the most part, that is, to a man on horseback and we decided that she must have taken shelter in some of them, for the trail disappeared suddenly after we got on some rocks.

We spent the greater part of the forenoon in endeavoring to penetrate those thickets and find some trace of her. There were cattle trails broken through most of them, but they were badly obstructed by brambles and partially broken branches of the live-oak and the stumps had no respect for one's person, nor the ribs and flanks of one's horse, so that it was necessary to traverse them slowly and with caution. Following one of them, when we had almost given her up, Puckett was in the lead, probably some twenty or thirty yards in front of me, when we discovered her.

It was not well to travel too close together, the branches the lead one pushed out of his way had a habit of flying back and were not particular where they caught the one behind and you were liable to lose an eye and in any case, they led to confusion. Well, as I remarked, we discovered her, or it would be more correct to say that she discovered us. For she suddenly burst from the thicket between us and took down the trail after Puckett for all she was worth.

She was not more than fifty feet in front of me, but Puckett never noticed her till I shouted. When I yelled to look out, that the bear was after him, he took a hurried glance over his shoulder and then sat down to ride. He was a heavy man, probably weighing 200 lbs or more, but the way he rode and quirted that horse to get the utmost out of him, would have qualified him for the Epsom Derby. It was nip and tuck, however, between him and the bear. She was right on his flank and casting hurried glances behind him, he made fresh exertions and rode more furiously.

I followed behind him to the best of my ability, rather overcome I regret to say with laughter. I expected the bear to catch up with him every minute, for the ground was not very suitable for a horse to run on, but the figures both of them cut were ludicrous. I had my gun in my hand, for I had taken it out of the scabbard to avoid the branches, but it was impossible to use it. The bear was so close behind him that any attempt to shoot her would more than likely have hit his horse and to shoot wild would endanger the rider.

Fortunately all things have an end, even Oxford Street and that clump of brush. When Puckett hit the open, intent on getting away from his pursuer, he swung his horse to the right, as rapidly as the pace he was going at would admit of. The bear, seeing him disappear round the corner, apparently was satisfied, for she kept straight on. Perhaps after all she only wanted to get away from us, or maybe she recognized Puckett as the aggressor of the previous day. Whatever it was she was evidently anxious to get away from us now and she would have done so, had we let her.

As soon as I got clear of the brush, I swung to the left and thus we had her between us and soon put an end to her. Our only excuse was that she was wounded, as we found on examination, in the foot evidently where I had hit her. The only mark we could find of Puckett's bullets was a decided abrasion on the point of the nose. It must have been that his last bullet had struck her there and knocked her out of time. A very fortunate shot for she was so close to him, that if she had not been stopped, she certainly would have mauled him, if no worse.

We skinned and dissected her where she was; she was in fair

condition and we packed the hide and a portion of her on one horse, with the remainder of the carcass on the other, which necessitated our leading them and gave us a long walk back to camp. Personally, I never had much use for bear meat and this was one of the few occasions on which I partook of it. The only other meat they had in camp was what the boys called sowbelly, nutritious no doubt but apt to pall on one as a steady diet.

Hunting Grizzlies in Chihuahua

Charles Sheldon

ca. 1890

Like his good friend, President Theodore Roosevelt, Charles Sheldon was not only a hunter and explorer—he devoted enormous energy to the fight for wildlife conservation. More than any other individual, Sheldon was responsible for the establishment of Mount McKinley National Park in Alaska, an area that he felt should be protected from mining operations and preserved for posterity. He was a central figure in the drafting and passage of legislation that resulted in the National Wildlife Refuge System and the Federal Duck Stamp required to take waterfowl. His comprehensive game code, adopted by the Territory of Alaska in 1924, was to serve as a model for progressive changes in the states of the "lower 48." Sheldon was also an accomplished and prolific writer, publishing books on his wilderness adventures in the upper Yukon (Scribner, 1911), the North Pacific Coast Islands (Scribner, 1912), Mount Denali in Alaska (Scribner, 1930) and the North American Southwest (Arizona Desert Bighorn Sheep Society, 1979).

While working on the El Paso–to–Chihuahua railroad, Sheldon was invited to invest in a Mexican silver and lead mining venture. On the collateral of his signature and Yale education, he was able to borrow $30,000 for investment capital. His investment proved sound, and Sheldon received a sufficient return from the mine to retire at age 36! Later, in 1909, Sheldon divested himself of his Mexican holdings, thus avoiding the financial losses that befell other American investors during the Díaz regime. He was thus free to spend the rest of his life exploring, hunting, and writing.

During his four years in Chihuahua (1898–1902), Sheldon was able to spend a great amount of time hunting, and it was during this period that his skills as a hunter-naturalist were honed. He also developed a conservation ethic that would long outlast his adventures in Mexico. Always a hunter, Sheldon realized early on that stringent measures would have to be instituted if his sport was to continue. The values of wild lands were especially important to Sheldon, and he became an outspoken advocate of wilderness areas. He makes a good case for the importance of both protection and wild lands in this account of Mexican grizzlies. Reading these passages gives us a sense of loss, however, for the grizzlies are no longer present in this locale.

Sheldon's recollections of his hunting experiences and wildlife observations in Chihuahua were published by the Boone and Crockett Club in 1925 in *Hunting in Conservation*, edited by Sheldon and George Bird Grinnell. The following account is from the chapter in that book entitled, "The Big Game of Chihuahua Mexico." 🌿

There was a charm in the hunting of this bear in the spring which was unique. About the first of May I used to camp in a clump of outlying pines on the plain. Two Mexican vaqueros, employed for general assistance, were my companions, or more precisely, good, well-tested friends. They always maintained the most friendly cheerfulness and genuine interest in the success of my trips. No amount of work ever diminished their happy spirits; more than anything else they enjoyed being out in camp, and all the vicissitudes of life in the wilderness. They never carried rifles or joined me in the actual hunting. One or the other would watch the horses all night and long before daylight he would arouse me from a healthy and profound sleep in the open air under the bright stars. I would then quickly set myself before a fire radiating its heat through the clear sharp air and have breakfast and coffee already prepared by my faithful friends. After their cheerful words wishing me good luck, I started walking rapidly across the plain, headed for the entrance to a canyon, which was reached before daylight. During the cooler hours of the morning the air always moved down these canyons; but after being well heated by the sun, its direction was reversed and it continued to move up all the afternoon. Should the day threaten to become very windy, either I did not start, or if a strong wind suddenly began to blow, immediately ceased hunting and returned. Except when the conditions were favorable, it was unwise to leave tracks in or disturb the hunting ground.

When objects could be clearly seen, I started slowly to walk up the canyon as noiselessly as possible, carefully watching ahead, continually pausing to look and listen. Most of these canyons, grading gently upward, are not rough; their bottoms, extending on both sides of a creek, are fairly level, and filled with a magnificent dense growth of tall pines, scattered madrono trees and patches of brush. Water seldom runs in the bed of the creek except near the head of the canyon. The pine-covered slopes on both sides incline upwards, gradually in some places, in others abruptly; but in a few places, for short distances only, the sides are walled in between high precipices.

It was not long before the sun came up and warmed the chill air, causing the spring love songs of the birds to sound on all sides. One of the most fascinating features of this section of the Sierra Madre is the wealth and variety of bird life in the early spring. The birds mass in the canyons and on the bordering slopes. Immediately trogons began calling from the trees, sweet warbler songs rose from all directions, sparrows and solitaires, robins and other birds, all joined in a chorus and added joy to the senses of the hunter. But my memory recalls most vividly the thousands of hummingbirds of several species, some of them brilliantly colored, filling the air, darting about everywhere, and the unceasing rhythm of their rapid wing beats and the thin chatter of their voices while in flight. Abert squirrels constantly scampered about the ground, turkeys were frequently seen; all nature seemed harmoniously to greet me while stealthily threading through the noble trees, my senses alert to every sound and sight around me.

I was well up the canyon, the sun was mounting higher, yet no signs of bears had been observed. But I kept on and on, never relaxing my caution, until finally several fresh bear tracks were seen in some exposed soil. An inspection of them showed that a bear had come down through the canyon to this point a couple of times and had returned almost in the same tracks. The head of the canyon was only a mile beyond and somewhere ahead a bear was regularly feeding on a carcass. Was I too late? Had the bear gone to rest? I did not believe it, because the canyon had been easy to find, good progress had been made, the direction of a slight breeze was favorable, and the hour was not too late. The cattle marks indicated more than one carcass, one of which might be found anywhere ahead. Caution was redoubled, the advance was selected toward any spot or elevation where a long sight ahead might be obtained. The cocked rifle was held ready for a possible quick shot. Short advances were maneuvered until a carcass was seen. Then a silent watch, long enough to be satisfied that no bear was near it. There were no signs indicating that one had been near it, and advancing up the canyon, until I noticed what seemed to be a sudden motion of something behind a patch of brush, I paused and watched, but detected no further movement. But not believing I had been deceived, step by step I moved to the right, for the purpose of reaching a slight elevation behind a tree where I could see beyond the brush. Finally I crept to the point and slowly rose. Near the brush, at a distance of a hundred yards, more or less, was a fine grizzly standing with its nose to the ground as if smelling the surface. A few yards away lay the carcass of a cow.

At the crack of the rifle, the bear fell, struggled a moment and died. It was a fine mature male, in beautiful full pelage of pale buffy color. Most of the hind quarters and part of one side of the cow's carcass had been eaten. The hour was nine. After a short rest I took the skin off, threw it over my shoulders and by noon the Mexicans, while cooking a good meal, were rejoicing at my success.

Later that day the camp was moved a couple of miles farther along the range to a point convenient for hunting another canyon. I did not find a bear in it the following morning, but crossed over a divide and followed down another canyon, where in the afternoon I killed a female bear as she was in the act of feeding. Three days later in another canyon, a third bear was killed, a dark male.

At times, however, bears were not found so quickly and several

canyons were hunted from different camps before success could be
attained. While shooting bear on these spring hunts, I had a variety of
interesting experiences with them, yet the description given is typical
of the methods of hunting at that season.

In the later part of May or early June, the bears ceased feeding on
carcasses and began widely to roam through the mountains, having
some preference for the great canyons. During the summer months
they could not often be methodically hunted. I traveled much
through these mountains in summer and in some sections usually saw
a grizzly or two, but never attempted to shoot one after the month of
May. I never found an authenticated case or reliable report of one of
these bears killing cattle. In fact, the Mexicans themselves, who continually ranged through the bear country looking for stock, maintained that grizzlies never molested live cattle, and that the latter did
not fear them. Johnny Bell also held the same decided opinions.

By fall the bears were very fat, and by October all had worked well
back within the mountains, where they always made their winter
dens. Here are wide valleys lying between the precipitous slopes of
high mountains on either side. In these valleys are long ridges covered
with acorn-bearing oaks. Here the grizzlies more or less assembled for
two or three weeks before hibernating, and fed on the nuts. Every fall
I made a special trip to hunt them, reaching the valley ridges after a
hunt for deer and turkeys. Afoot and alone, I tramped over the ridges
and always saw several bears, some of which I never failed to secure.
Because the bears, while feeding, kept actively moving over wide
areas, hard, vigorous hunting was necessary to get a good shot at one,
and often I was obliged to stalk for hours. But it was a fine sport in a
magnificent country. Although I frequently traveled through the
mountains in winter, I never saw signs of bears during the months of
hibernation. But Mexicans who had spent most of their lives in or
near the mountains, and also Johnny Bell, told me that during warmer
days in winter, bears often wandered about for short distances from
their dens. I have no doubt it is true. Every year, including spring and
fall hunts, I shot five or six grizzlies.

Now that a railroad follows the edge of the mountains, and mines
and lumber mills have invaded this habitat of the bears, they are

greatly reduced in numbers, and their range is restricted to smaller areas far within the sierra; the sport which I enjoyed is gone forever. They are following their relatives in the United States along the path to extinction. This will happen before a long period of time. Then, although the glory of the scenery in the Sierra Madre will remain, complete enjoyment of the spirit of these mountains will have vanished. The deep, mysterious emotions aroused by the sight of, or by a sense of the presence of, the grizzly bear in the wilderness will be lacking.

PART II

Things Get Ugly

The Age of Conflict, 1884–1925

Looking into the Gila Wilderness Area of New Mexico. In this great bear country and in Arizona's Blue Range Primitive Area, grizzlies persisted into the 1930s. Photograph by David E. Brown.

A Bear Hunter Who Lost

Albert E. Thompson

1885

There are several versions of Wilson's death from a grizzly near Indian Gardens on Arizona's now bustling Oak Creek. The story was told and retold, and it is not surprising that each version differs in detail, particularly in regard to Wilson's character and who found his body. The following "family account" by Albert E. Thompson, published by the Sedona Westerners in *Those Early Days . . . Oldtimers' Memoirs* in 1968, was selected as the most readable and "matter of fact." Although this rendition was published many years after the event and makes no mention of Wilson's eccentric and colorful partner, "Bear Howard," the particulars are based on the records of the Coroner's inquest conducted at the "scene of the killing." As to the cause of Wilson's demise, all versions agree—even to the species of tree from which the bear pulled him down.

The story illustrates how the few deaths by grizzly in the Southwest were preceded—almost invariably—by a man taking on a bear single-handed and with an inadequate weapon. Perhaps just as informative is the insight gained into the homesteader's life. People living such a life of boredom and loneliness had little sympathy for bears and, in fact, competed with the animals for a livelihood. No wonder that bears were killed at every opportunity. 🌿

In the Spring of 1885, John James Thompson and his young wife and two small children were living in a log cabin on the present George Jordan ranch in what is now Sedona, Arizona.

He had taken squatter's rights to a claim at Indian Gardens, four miles farther up the creek some ten years previous. The Indian Gardens ranch was in such wild country and so inaccessible, he had built the cabin at the Jordan ranch when he married, so his wife could be near her parents. They lived on the present Fred Hart ranch, about two miles down the creek.

The previous year, Mr. Thompson had taken a temporary partner to help him farm the Indian Gardens ranch. He was an old Arkansas bear hunter, by the name of Richard Wilson. He first came to Tucson, Arizona in 1864. Mr Wilson and a man named Jim Woolsy had built a neat hewed log cabin at Indian Gardens, but Wilson himself, camped in a hut about a half mile from the cabin.

In June 1885, Mr. Thompson was called as a witness in a court case of some kind to Prescott, the County Seat. (Remember, at that time, Coconino County had not been made from part of Yavapai. Yavapai County extended to the Utah border.)

Mrs. Thompson's family had moved from Sedona with their cattle to the mountains for the Summer. Mr. Thompson did not like to leave his wife and small children alone while he was gone to Prescott, so he asked Mr. Wilson to come down every evening while he was gone and spend the night near the family.

Mr. Wilson had been telling Thompson about seeing the tracks of a monstrous grizzly bear between Sedona and Indian Gardens. He said he intended to kill the big bear. He had broken the sight on his large calibre bear gun and had only a small rifle to use. He asked Thompson to take his big rifle to Prescott and have the sights repaired. Thompson told him to leave the big bear absolutely alone until he got back from Prescott with the big rifle and the old man agreed to do so.

The evening of the very day that Mr. Thompson left home, Mr. Wilson failed to show up at the Thompson cabin in Sedona. Not only did he fail to appear the first evening, but for eight days Mrs. Thompson and the two little children, a boy of three and a girl of one

year, were alone. The nearest neighbor was about five miles away by
trail down the creek.

Mrs. Thompson said later that she was both worried and frightened, but she was almost helpless to do anything about her plight.
She did not even have a horse. The only livestock she had were milk
cows and pigs. She had to tend the stock and rustle wood for cooking
and carry water from the creek for house use and for the pigs.

On the ninth day she was happy to see two men riding in on
horseback. They were Judge John Goodwin and his son Tom from
Jerome. They asked Mrs. Thompson for the key to the cabin at Indian
Gardens, as they wanted to spend a few days trout fishing there. They
were old friends of the Thompsons, and Mrs. Thompson said she
would be glad to let them have the key, but Mr. Wilson had it. She
told them that she was dreadfully worried for fear that something
serious had happened to Mr. Wilson or he would not have stayed
away so long.

Judge Goodwin tried to reassure her by telling her that Wilson had
just got busy with his farm work and forgotten his promise to come
down of evenings.

Mrs. Thompson stoutly denied that and insisted that Mr. Wilson
was an honest and trustworthy man and would not have broken his
promise if it had been humanly possible for him to keep it.

The Judge told her that he and his son would ride on up the
canyon and investigate and come back and let her know what they
had found out.

As Mrs. Thompson used to tell it,—"They had been gone for only
a short while when she saw them coming back, riding pretty fast." She
knew they had bad news.

They had got only as far as Wilson Canyon. It is the big canyon
that Highway 89A now crosses over Midgley Bridge near where it
enters Oak Creek. It is about half way between Sedona and Indian
Gardens.

The old trail used to cross the canyon much farther up in the hills.
The Goodwins had crossed the canyon and started up the steep north
side when they heard a dog bark. They went back to the bottom of the
canyon, past the forks and up the left hand branch into a box canyon

with a high cliff fall ahead. There they had found the battered body of
Wilson, the bear hunter. His faithful dog was still with him.

The Goodwins came immediately back to the Thompson cabin
and reported what they had found. Judge Goodwin then sent his son
Tom, back to Jerome for help. He told Mrs. Thompson that he would
stay with her because he knew she had already had it plenty rough,
being marooned there alone. She was very grateful for the offer. Tom
went to Jerome and brought back enough men to hold a Coroner's
inquest at the scene of the killing. The Judge, being the Justice of the
Peace at Jerome, presided at the inquest.

The story, pieced out at the inquest, and from what Mrs. Thompson could tell them is as follows: Mr. Wilson had quit work early
enough in the evening to get to the Thompson cabin before dark. He
had two pack burros that he had loaded with little potatoes for feed
for the pigs at Thompsons.

Apparently he and Mr. Thompson had dug potatoes previously
and packed the marketable ones out and Thompson had taken them
to market in Prescott.

It appeared that Wilson had got as far on his way as Wilson
Canyon. (Of course it did not have that name then.) He caught sight
of the big bear there. In spite of the fact that he had only a light rifle
and a young untrained dog, he could not resist the temptation to kill
it. He, an old experienced bear hunter, had lost all fear of the big
brutes. He shot the bear and wounded it. Very foolishly he followed it
up a brushy canyon with an untrained dog.

It appeared from sign that the bear had gone up the box canyon
and stopped in a brush thicket. The hunter followed it by tracks and
dripping blood, expecting to get another shot and kill it. He stepped
past some Arizona Cypress trees and the bear jumped at him so close
he had no chance. He ran for a tree and dropped his gun. He tried to
climb the tree but the bear caught him by the heel of his shoe and
pulled him down. He was wearing heavy hob-nailed mountaineer
shoes. One shoe had the heel almost pulled off and showed the marks
of the bear's teeth. The Cypress tree that he had tried to climb had a
limb almost as thick as a man's wrist almost twisted off. It showed
how desperately the old hunter had clung to the tree to try to save his
life.

The body was found some ten or fifteen feet from the tree. It was lying face down in a little pool of water. It appeared that the bear had pulled the hunter from the tree and either bitten part of his face off or knocked it off with his paw. The belief was that the bear had then gone away. The hunter had then regained consciousness and crawled to the pool of water to try to get a drink. He had passed out again and fallen in the water and drowned. At least that is what the jury decided from the evidence at hand.

The old man's body was too badly decomposed to move any great distance. Bed rock was too near the surface to dig a very deep grave. They just wrapped him in his blankets and buried him in a shallow grave and piled a big mound of boulders on top of his grave. At the base of the cliff they cut his initials, R. W., into the rock.

The old man's burros were found grazing on the slope of the mountain north of there. They had torn holes in the potato sacks and scattered little potatoes far and wide, but still had part of the pack rigs on them.

When Mr. Thompson returned from Prescott, his old friend and partner was dead and buried.

Some years later, some of the old man's friends from Jerome dug up the bones and reburied them at the Thompson ranch at Indian Gardens, where they have lain all these years.

Some fifteen years after the killing, Frank Thompson, who was the little three year old boy when Wilson was killed, found the skeleton of a very large bear in high brush near the top of Wilson Mountain, some two miles from the scene of the killing. He brought the bear's skull home to his father's house. His father asked him if he had looked for Wilson's hunting knife there. He went back several weeks later but could never find the skeleton again. As it was never found, Thompson always believed that the old man had stuck it in the bear and the bear had carried it away with him and died from his wounds,—but we will never know.

Encounter with a Bear

George C. Naegle

1892

The following is an eyewitness account of the last of the few deaths by
a grizzly in the Southwest. The story is unquestionably true; it was
reported far and wide. Both E. W. Nelson of the U. S. Biological
Survey and the naturalist, Charles Sheldon, heard about the incident
while in Chihuahua and reported some of the particulars.

Now, thanks to Tom Whetten and Ron McKinnon of Tucson, this
letter, written immediately after the "attack," is available for all to
read. The events leading up to poor Hyrum's death follow a familiar
pattern—while protecting free-ranging stock in a wilderness of large
predators, a bear is taken on and pressed too close with an insufficient
firearm. The bear's method of mauling the victim and the nature of
the wounds are characteristic of most grizzly attacks.

The grizzly did not survive much longer in Mexico's Sierra Madre.
Expeditions to the Colonia Pacheco and other Sierra Madre locales by
A. S. Leopold and his staff found no one who knew of grizzlies
inhabiting these areas after 1920, despite the fact that Mormon
hunters from Colonia Pacheco had been able to supply E. W. Nelson
and A. E. Goldman with a series of specimens for the U. S. National
Museum at about the time of the Naegle incident. Rumors of grizzlies in the area persist to this day, but they are campfire talk, not hard
evidence. ❧

My dear brother and sister, Joseph and Frances, Toquerville, Wash. Co., U.T.:

This letter will surely be a shock and surprise to you and the members of our family in Utah and Arizona, and the pen will but feebly convey to you the sad intelligence of the fate of our dear brother Hyrum, who, from the horrible wounds inflicted by an enraged bear, died last night at 10 o'clock. This news will cause you to feel with us the bitter pangs of grief at his untimely death. I now send you the whole circumstances: Nearly all winter some of us boys have gone to the valley about fifteen miles from here, west, over the mountain on the Sonora side of the Sierra Madres, to the ranch. There we would stay the week and return home on Saturday night. On account of being so busy, and as father and some of the boys were over at the new purchase in Sonora, we were usually there only one at a time to look out for the stock, and especially to save the calves and colts from the bears, mountain lions and big grey wolves, which have been very destructive this spring. Already over three hundred dollars' worth have been lost. Brother Hyrum came home on Saturday night and said he had encountered a bear but did not get him. He also reported tracks quite thick; so we both went over last Monday; on Tuesday we hunted in different directions, and found several of our best calves gone. Then we decided to go together next day down the river Gabalan [Gavilán], back up North Creek, and gather up all the cows and calves. I believe that was the first day any of us had ridden together, the day through, during nearly the entire spring, and even when two were there we would ride in different directions, so as to get around among the stock and over more country. As we came up North Creek driving a little bunch of cattle, on turning a curve in the canyon and emerging from the point of a hill, Hyrum exclaimed, "There's a bear!" It was a monster, too. Instantly we jerked our guns and leaped to the ground. Hyrum had a 44-Winchester and I a 45-70 Marlin. We ran a few paces to a clearing where we had a full view and a fair chance at him. As bruin was going along the bottom of the canyon, Hyrum put in the first shot, and I the next, both hitting him. In rapid succession we fired several shots and I think most of them struck the brute. As he climbed the hill on the opposite side, my third shot brought him rolling and bawling down the hill.

Hyrum said, "that's cooked him," but he only lay a second and gathering himself up he scrambled to the top of the hill for about twenty or thirty yards and fell under an oak. Hyrum suggested, "Let's take it afoot," and started after him, but having only three cartridges in my magazine, in the haste and excitement of trying to put in more, unfortunately, the first one caught fast, and I could neither force it in nor out until I got my pocket knife. By that time Hyrum was across the creek and climbing the hill, following the bear. I looked up and shouted to him not to follow directly after the brute, but to come in below him, take straight up the hill and come out above or on a level with him. He did so, and as soon as he reached the top he fired three shots, bang! bang! bang! as quickly as he could. I think the bear must have been on the run while he was shooting, and with the third shot got out of sight over a little raise. In the hurry to adjust my gun and go there I did not look up again till I got the discharged cartridge out and others in. Both Hyrum and the monster being then out of sight, I jumped on my mule—a fleet little animal—and with gun in hand dashed across the canyon. Fortunately I did, for had I taken the journey afoot, I should have reached there too late, for when I arrived on the top of the hill I could not see nor hear anything of them. I called, "Hyrum, Hyrum, where are you?" but received no answer, and sped on the course I thought they had gone but a few rods over a little raise, when I saw the bear above and a little along the hill side, but I could see no Hyrum. Rushing toward the bear, I could see that he had something bloody in his mouth, munching and growling. Not seeing Hyrum anywhere I feared he had him down, and my horror no human tongue can tell when I first saw his blue overall under the bears body. He was gnawing Hyrum's hand. I shrieked: "My Lord! My Lord! has he got brother Hyrum." The spurring up of my mule caused the brute to drop the hand and pick up his head. For fear of making an accidental shot and hitting Hyrum, or perchance the shot might not prove fatal to the bear, I jumped off to make sure aim. Being then quite close, my jump to the ground frightened him, or at least instead of touching Hyrum again, or making for me before I could level down to shoot, he started off. Hyrum rolled over on his face and rose on his knees and elbows. Then I could see my brother was not dead, but oh! such a bloody sight I am unable to describe. The bear was then about thirty yards from him. I fired and brought the brute to the ground, but he got up and started again. A second shot, however, brought him tumbling again, this time to get up and turn on me; but as he turned he fell, and grabbed in his mouth a dry pine limb about the size of my arm. That he crunched as though it were a cornstalk, and with it in his mouth he started off again. A third shot brought him writhing to the earth, and as my last cartridge was in the barrel I proceeded within six feet of his head and sent it through the brain of the huge brown bear. I then rushed back to Hyrum. All this was done in half the time it takes to relate.

Now came the trying ordeal for myself. There alone, with Hyrum's mangled body, fifteen miles away from home and help, how I cried and prayed. The poor boy was still resting on his knees and elbows, with the blood entirely covering his head, face and shoulders and still streaming to the ground. The first thing I did was to support his head and administer to him, after which he cried, "Water." I galloped to the creek and brought my hat full of water, and washed his head and face the best I could. Such a mangled head and face you never saw. The skull was laid bare from the top of the fore-head about four inches back, and there was one wound on the left side, three-cornered, about two inches each way and one other wound that we did not discover until just before his death, when some portions of his brain oozed out, two teeth having penetrated the brain. On the back and other side of his head, and just at the corner of his right eye, were seven or eight terribly ugly gashes laying bare the skull. There was a long gash down the right cheek and two under the jaw, which was washed; his upper lip was half torn off. In all, there were twenty wounds on his head, face, and the right hand was chewed through and through; his left was bitten through in several places; there was one fearful bite on the left leg, just above the knee, and one heavy imprint of the bear's paw and claws, though not deep, on the right breast. Of course these wounds on his body were not observable at first, but I could see his critical state, and knowing that God alone could help us in our lonely

and helpless condition, I told Hyrum to exercise all the faith he had
strength to do and I would again administer to him. After this he
spoke, and I asked him why he went so near the monster. He said the
bear got over a little raise out of sight and was lying down, and he did
not see him until within two rods, when the bear sprung up and after
him. His gun would not go off, though he kept it leveled on the brute,
thinking every second it would act. When the beast was nearly upon
him he started backwards, still trying to pull the trigger, but it failed.
The bear struck him with his left paw, the right one being disabled,
breaking his jaw and knocking him down. The bear then jumped on
him, grabbed him by the head with his mouth; and to protect his
head and face he put up his hands.

About eight feet from where my brother lay I found his hat and
gun. The latter was cocked and contained three cartridges. I think, in
the excitement, he failed to press the lever, and that accounted for its
not going off.

After tying up his broken jaw and getting him on his horse (which
I led), to my astonishment he rode a mile and a half to camp where I
laid him upon the bed and washed and dressed his wounds, bandaged
them in salt water cloths and gave him a little milk and cold water to
revive him, as he had swooned a couple of times from loss of blood.
He rallied and I asked him what I should do—go for help, or try to
get him home. He replied, "don't leave me here alone," and the
thought to myself of leaving him while I rode fifteen miles over a very
rough trail and returned with help could not be entertained. Again,
such a thing as Hyrum riding so far in such a condition could not be
hoped for nor expected. But to my astonishment he had, by the help
of God, ridden one and a half miles, and I told him that same God,
and He only, could give him support and strength to reach home, and
if he thought he could stand the ride we would make a start at once.
So I quickly saddled him a fresh horse, and provided myself with a
two-gallon syrup can of water (which I replenished at Bear Spring),
and with a cup and spoon. I put my coat and a slicker on him, as it was
cloudy and threatened rain. Then for the third time I administered to
him, helped him in the saddle, made a roll of a pair of blankets and a
heavy camp quilt to put in front of him to support him, as I thought I

would have to use these for a bed for him before reaching home. We started at a fast walk, I driving his horse along the trail, he handling the reigns with his left arm. This went on till dark; then I led the horse through the timber and over the mountain, and by giving him every few moments a little water, which he called for, I arrived with him at his home at 10 o'clock at night, the accident having happened about 3 p.m. on Wednesday, the 22nd.

In passing through our little town I called up Patriarch Henry Lunt to get others to assist in administering to him and dressing his wounds. I sent for Franklin Scott, his father-in-law, who sewed up the worst of the wounds, and also Sister O. C. Moffatt to assist in caring for him, and we continued from that time to apply every remedy within our reach to allay fever and keep out inflammation, etc. We also sent word to Apostle Thatcher to come and have the doctor from Carolites sent for. We continued our prayers and supplications for Hyrum's recovery. To all appearance and to the astonishment of every one who saw him, he went on well until yesterday, when about the same time in the p.m. that he was hurt he was taken worse and had quite a bad spell of vomiting. His breathing became heavy and difficult, and the brain began to ooze from two of the gashes in the head. He gradually sank, until just before his noble spirit fled he made a great effort to throw off the accumulation from his lungs. With two or three deep gasps he opened his left eye (which was not hurt), and looked as if to say "Good-bye," and died calmly and peacefully. I think he was conscious to the last, and endured his suffering manfully, patiently and without a murmur.

To endure such a ride in his condition was characteristic of his extraordinarily strong constitution. Not a groan nor a sound did he make while the bear was on him; and not one man in one hundred, perhaps not in five hundred, could have borne what he did without complaint. The grief of those of the family who surrounded him at his death, and especially the anguish of his young wife was most heart-rending. Hyrum was only married in January last. He was 23 and his widow is 19.

I desire to add our gratitude to our Heavenly Father for His tender mercy in bearing him to his home, wife and family; it is a marvel to all how I got home with him. I tell them nothing but the power of God supported him to reach here.

Poor Hyrum has a record in the Mexican mission that will be a monument of honor to him. He was president of the Deacons Quorum for a while, and was up to the time of his death, an acting priest and one of my counselors in the M. I. A.

I remain, in sympathy and affection, your Brother,

Geo. C. Naegle.
Colonia Pacheco, Chihuahua, Mexico
June 25, 1892

Bear Cosper and
Fred Fritz's Bear Fights

*as told by J. T. Mathews
and Joseph Miller*

1907

Back in the mid-1960s a group of Arizona Game and Fish Department men were camped in the White Mountains and telling bear stories around the campfire; naturally, the talk soon turned to grizzlies. The senior editor, then a greenhorn Wildlife Manager, spoke out to bemoan the fact that there were now no more grizzly tales to relate. Wasn't it a shame, he asked, that our predecessors had killed them off? In answer, one of the veterans of the party, Phil Cosper, turned and stalked off. Bob White, Regional Supervisor for Region I (Pinetop), then spoke up: "You had better watch what you say about grizzlies around Phil. His grandfather was almost killed by one and at least one other of his relatives spent most of his life getting rid of them."

Years later the story was related of how Phil's maternal grandfather, Fred Fritz, Sr., had come upon a big grizzly, which had mauled him so badly that he never fully recovered from his wounds. His later days, before he died at the relatively young age of 55, were spent sleeping on pillows saturated in alcohol to relieve the pain. Another often told story was how Phil's other grandfather, Tole, also known as "Bear" Cosper, had a lifelong vendetta against bears and was said to have "regularly killed a bear for breakfast"—hence the nickname.

Unlike many campfire stories, both of these word-of-mouth accounts were substantiated by an earlier written version with few discrepancies in the details. A gentleman named Mathews had summarized Tole Cosper's bear-bashing feats in a 1907 letter to the *Clifton Copper Era*, following an account in that newspaper of Fred Fritz's escape from a grizzly in 1905. These two stories were later republished with other newspaper clips of that era by Joseph Miller in his 1956 book, *Arizona: The Last Frontier* (Hastings House, New York). Both Mathews's "letter to the editor" and Fritz's article were again reprinted in *Arizona Bear Fights*, by B. D. Haynes and E. Haynes (1979), in their marvelous anthology, *The Grizzly Bear: Portraits From Life.*

The exploits of these reckless cowmen make us wonder why more men weren't killed by grizzlies and how the animals were able to persist as long as they did.

First, Mathews's rundown on Bear Cosper. 🐾

J. H. T. Cosper, better known as Tole Cosper, bears the reputation of having killed more bears than any other man in the Blue country. His ranch and range lies on and adjacent to the Blue range, a wild and rugged country, with deep canyons and high hills whose slopes are covered with dense thickets of pine and underbrush. Many bears inhabit these canyons and forests, and Cosper's work frequently brings him in contact with them. He seems to have an eye for bears. His luck at finding them is phenomenal, and rarely do the soft-nose bullets from his thirty-forty fail to do deadly work. But even a thirty-forty does not kill every time, and Cosper has had many narrow escapes with enraged and wounded bears.

Some years ago when in a bear fight and while trying to protect a boy from a wounded bear that was pursuing him, Cosper rode too near the bear. The desperate animal unable to stand the fire from behind, suddenly wheeled, charged Cosper, and leaped upon his horse, and in another instant would have torn him to pieces had not a well-directed bullet broken his jaw and sent him reeling to the ground.

Last fall while riding along a lonely trail on the Blue range, a huge silvertip suddenly appeared in the path not over forty yards away, and insisted on the right-of-way. While the bear stood sizing him up, Cosper quietly dismounted, took deliberate aim and began "fogging" him. Although the first bullet dealt him a mortal wound, the bear uttered a savage roar and made for his enemy. His horse took fright and fled, and Cosper, thinking discretion the better part of valor, tried to fly up a pine tree, but ere he could climb beyond his reach, the bear was almost upon him and would have caught him had not the snorting and plunging of his horse attracted bruin's attention for a moment. As the bear turned to the horse, the hunter seized the opportunity and while holding to the tree with one hand fired his gun with the other, breaking the bear's neck. When he descended and examined his gun, there was only one cartridge left in the magazine. The bear weighed about seven hundred pounds.

Unless wounded, a bear rarely shows fight, but either runs or stands curiously eyeing the hunter, but occasionally and especially when hungry, a bear will assume the offensive.

Last May, Cosper, his two sons and Charles Chapman were "rimming" for cattle in Stray Horse, a deep canyon that heads on the Blue range. When they reached Rose Peak, a high mountain near the head of the canyon, they stopped to rest their horses and while seated on a log Chapman jestingly remarked that he wished seven hundred bears would charge them. The others laughed and expressed their opinions as to how quickly he could ascend a tree in case even one should happen along. Scarcely had their laughter died away when a hoarse growl told them his wish had come to pass. They scarcely had time to snatch their guns from the scabbards, when a huge silvertip appeared in the trail above them not twenty yards away, making straight for them. Four rifles spouted forth and sent death-dealing missiles into his body, but the bear was not checked until he was almost upon them and a dozen bullets had entered his body, one going down his windpipe and through his heart. Had it been one man instead of four, nothing but a lucky shot could have saved him from death. This bear weighed fully eight hundred pounds. He measured eight feet from his nose to tail and the hide when spread out measured nine feet across from the front paw to the hind paw.

Mr. Editor, if you ever want to go on a bear hunt, go with Cosper, and there will be "something doing."

Yours very truly,
J. T. Mathews

Miller's Account of Fred Fritz's Bear Fight

While riding his range in the neighborhood of Maple Springs, he cut the trail of a bear, which was nothing unusual in that section. He had four dogs with him and a pistol; hence he did not hesitate to follow the trail, feeling certain that he would have little trouble in dispatching bruin. Fritz had killed many bears previous to this time without an experience worth reporting. But this bear was different. He was not only big, old and tough, but also a fighter. He trailed the old fellow only a short distance when he was overtaken in some pinon timber. Fritz opened fire with his pistol. The dogs also took an interest in the fight, but the bear did not apparently take an interest in them, but he made a break for Fritz, and being on higher ground he jumped partly onto the horse and grabbed him with his mouth and claws. Fritz then got another shot which broke the bear's jaw, and caused him to relax his hold on the horse. He then emptied his revolver at the bear thinking he would settle him, but owing to the fact that the horse was fractious and the bear's hide tough, he was not able to land a fatal shot. He rode off a short distance and reloaded, and then discovered that he had only six cartridges. In the meantime the dogs were following bruin and worrying him greatly. He then took up the trail, and after following it about a mile overtook the bear in a narrow canyon. He dismounted from his horse and followed the bear up into some sharp rocks, and just as he was surmounting one of them, the bear jumped onto him and together they rolled down several feet, the bear landing on top. Fritz landed face downward. He was somewhat stunned by the fall, but was quickly brought to his senses by the bear taking the back of his head in its mouth, and had it not been for the fact that the brute's jaw had previously been broken, no doubt the battle would have ended in favor of bruin.

Fritz managed to get his gun into action and firing over his shoulder caught the bear in the mouth, the bullet coming out at the butt of his ear. Ordinarily this should have ended the fight, but not so in this case. The bear apparently realizing that he could not use his mouth effectively proceeded with his claws to tear the leather "chaps" off of the now almost helpless man. This turned him over and he was again able to use his pistol, which he did until every shot had been fired. The dogs again took an interest in the fight, and attracted bruin's attention, but every time Fritz attempted to get up the bear came back and sat upon him while slapping at the dogs. He used the pistol as a club and broke it. He then managed to get out his pocket knife, which was so small and light that it would not penetrate through the tough hide of the bear. Fritz then realized that his only show of escape was through the dogs, and he encouraged them in their attack, and in this manner, more dead than alive, with his clothes almost torn off, and bloody from head to foot, he managed to reach his horse. At this time, his nephew, who had heard the shooting, arrived on the scene, and the two men followed the bear who was dragging the dogs with him. When they overtook the bear they saw that he was very sick. The nephew took one shot at him, and the bear afterwards died. Fritz had laid up at his ranch for many days, and will carry the scars of the battle with him to the grave. When the bear was skinned seven bullets were found in his body.

Bear Moore's Life-Scars

Jack Stockbridge

ca. early 1900s

Both Jack Stockbridge and Bear Moore are important figures in the early history of the country now known as the Gila Wilderness. A chronicler of the region's pioneer life, Jack Stockbridge's account of Bear Moore first appeared in Elizabeth McFarland's *Wilderness of the Gila*, an anthology published by the University of New Mexico Press in 1974. Stockbridge came into the region in 1900. The rest of his life he spent prospecting and hunting in the Gila headwaters. Here he relates what he knows about Bear Moore, probably one of the most eccentric and deranged figures to ever live in the Southwest. No one will ever know how many bears Moore put to slow, cruel death in order to "settle the score" after he had been attacked and mauled.[1] The small populations of grizzlies in the Southwest could not withstand such pressures and eventually disappeared. Such bizarre incidents persist. In Lycoming County, Pennsylvania, a man was charged in 1985 with killing and mutilating at least ten black bears, a sad commentary on humankind's relations with bears. 🐾

---

[1]For additional information on Moore, the reader is referred to J. E. Hawley's recollections of Bear Moore driving heated rods into a bear captured in a "cabin trap" in *The Grizzly in the Southwest* by David E. Brown, published by the University of Oklahoma Press in 1985.

I met Bear Moore for the first time when Merrill and I made our first trip to Turkey Creek in 1900. Bear Moore was turning gray and looked to be fifty or sixty years old then. He was real unfriendly and threatening even, and we thought he might be dangerous. So Merrill and I just gave up on prospecting around there for the time being. We went to hunting instead. There was a good many bear in the country then.

Merrill and I killed several bear and dressed the hides and fixed them up pretty nice. To preserve the hides, we would take them over to Alum Mountain where there was a solid bunch of pure alum. A German outfit, Doctor Sauer and his son Maynard and some other men, had a camp at Alum Mountain on the Gila River, where there's a little warm spring, a sort of a nice place. They had patented some forty-odd claims and were driving tunnels into the hills. Capillary action would bring out the alum in these tunnels and we would find chunks of pure stuff. We would put that alum on the bear hides to preserve them. Later we took them over to the Gila Hot Springs and the Hill brothers would sell the hides for us to people coming in to the springs.

Next time I saw Bear Moore was in 1903, when Lee Meader and I made our circuit around the Wilderness. When we went up Turkey Creek, Bear Moore was camped in his cave there. The old man had been washing and had his jacket off. I never knew him to wear anything but a long jacket and old blue levi overalls and a pair of shoes—no underclothing even in cold weather.

We could see scars all over his body and Lee keeps staring at him and starts to ask him some questions. Old Moore wouldn't answer him and I says to Lee, "Well, let's go up this canyon and camp there. I know of a good place to camp." I knew old Bear Moore was liable to say something to Lee that he wouldn't like.

After we got our camp set up, pretty soon Lee says, "Well, let's go down and talk to that old man a little bit."

I says, "Well, all right if you want to."

So we went down to Bear Moore's cave. Lee wanted to find out all about Moore's fight with a bear in the San Mateos, but old man Moore wouldn't talk about it and acted real peculiar. We went back to our camp and Lee says, "Well, the old devil, he's crazy all right!" After awhile I told Lee, "I'm going down and see if the old feller needs anything. No use you going along."

He says, "No. I know it. He won't talk if I'm along."

I went back to the cave by myself and spent three or four hours talking with old Bear Moore. Later when I was Forest Ranger for that whole area, I run across him now and then, and for the next ten years until I left that part of the country. I even camped with him a time or two. He would talk to me if I was by myself. I guess he talked to me as much as to anybody. He told me his name was James Moore and he had come into the Gila country in the early eighties when the soldiers was chasing Geronimo and had camped up in the Mogollons. He had spent a lot of time with the soldiers. In the winter he used to stay at the Gila Hot Springs and put in his time hunting in the mountains round about. He'd kill a deer and that would last him for quite a while. He said he never did eat anything much.

He also told me about when the bear eat him up. You can hear a dozen different stories about that. There was the story in *Argosy* magazine that told a whole lot of stuff about it. It's absolutely wrong for every word. This was what really happened according to what Bear Moore himself told me:

"In 1892 I'd gone over in the San Mateos to see a friend. I always used one of them old Sharp's 45-70 single shot rifles. About a mile from the cabin where I was staying, I went hunting with that old rifle and I run onto a little young bear up a tree. I shot it but didn't kill it, and it squawked and fell out of that tree.

"About that time here comes the old bear. I went to jump back out of the way and fell backwards over a log with the bear right on top of me. As I fell, I lost my gun, but I always carry a bowie knife. Me and that bear had it right there. The bear got a hold of me and bit me through the jaws and on my forehead and through my arms and clawed me acrost the breast. That bear just darn near chewed me up and spit me out.

"I managed to kill the bear with my bowie knife, and crawled back a mile to the cabin where my friend was. He taken me in to Magdalena to the hospital and they patched me up there as best they could. My face was left all twisted out to one side and I never shaved after that. I can't talk very plain either. There's scars on my forehead and arms, and you can see my heart beat where that bear clawed my chest open. When I was able, they sent me back to my home in Missouri and I stayed there until I was cured up enough to come back out here again. Ever since, they've always called me Bear Moore."

I guess Bear Moore was loco in a way, from thinking about that bear that nearly killed him and left him scarred for the rest of his life. Through the years he kept building bear traps. I found several—half a dozen maybe—around the Mogollon country. He made them out of logs—good, stout logs, some a foot in diameter, I guess. I don't know how the devil the old feller rolled them up together. He would make a trap door out of a big tree he would cut down. The door had to be about three feet wide, big enough for a big bear to get in.

I had seen the bear traps around there and I'd heard that he killed the bears—murdered them—in the traps. Once I was going through Little Turkey Park, where Little Turkey runs into Little Creek on the other side of Big Turkey. Bear Moore had a camp there. I heard the durndest racket down in the canyon. I listened a little bit, and it was Bear Moore a-swearing and a-cussing and an old bear growling and just raising Cain. Between them they made a devil of a noise.

I rode down and there was Bear Moore with a bowie knife tied onto a stout stick, poking between the logs of a trap at the bear caught in it. All the time he was cussing the bear. He says, "Oh, you will eat a man up, will you!" and then he'd cuss some more. And he kept on that way until he killed the bear. The bear hide wasn't no good after that—all full of holes.

Most of the time Bear Moore stayed in his camp at Little Turkey Park or at his cave on Turkey Creek. One year Bear Moore got hold of some hogs and drove them over towards Turkey Creek. The hillside there is covered with great big white oak trees and there's lots of acorns. It come a snowstorm and the hogs like to froze to death, but he finally got them out over to the West Fork of the Gila. There's a little bottom land down below the mouth of White Creek on the West Fork. There Bear Moore built a cabin of log blocks against the bluff. He left port-holes between the blocks because there was still some

Apaches around in the Mogollons. He raised some pumpkins and corn and quite a little stuff like that.

That's wild rocky country without any trail in the West Fork, but there was one place where Bear Moore could get down from the west side. That's the Ring Canyon trail from McKenna Park. Bear Moore got to looking around and he found a pretty good quartz vein that runs out through Ring Canyon and breaks out into red bluffs right across the West Fork from Chicken Coop Canyon.

By climbing down there five or six hundred feet with a rope, he could get some high-grade red hematite ore. But he would have to get the ore out of there and take it to his cabin to pan it. Bear Moore got kind of uneasy about going down that rope and monkeying around there with nobody to help. But he didn't want to tell no big bugs about his find, so he goes over to the Montoya place at the mouth of Diamond Creek.

Montoya was an old Mexican rancher who talked good English. He's the one who told me about this. He had a boy about twelve years old. Bear Moore gets this boy to come over and camp with him. The boy would stay up on top while Bear Moore went down and got the ore dirt in sacks, then the boy would pull it up for him.

They run along like that for three or four months till the weather began to get bad—winter coming. I think the boy got sick—anyway, he had to go home. For his pay Moore gives the boy a little Vaseline bottle with five or six ounces of gold in it. Montoya tried to find out from his boy where the gold came from, and the boy promised to take him up and show him. But the boy took sick from a cold and didn't live very long after Bear Moore had taken him home.

In winter it's pretty hard to get out of that West Fork country where Bear Moore's cabin was, so he would spend most of the winter at a cave over on Big Sycamore where it runs off into the Gila below Alum Mountain. From there, Moore would go into Pinos Altos and stay at Bill and Charlie Rathbun's place on Bear Creek. They had some mining claims there, and Bear Moore would do a little placering and take his gold in with theirs to sell at the Pinos Altos store.

PART III

Mopping Up
The Age of Professionals, 1913–1935

Ben Lilly in his later years on the G.O.S. Ranch, New Mexico. Photograph by Norm Woolsey.

My Biggest Grizzly

Ben V. Lilly

1913

To speak of bears in the Southwest is to speak, sooner or later, of Ben Lilly—the Southwest's most famous outdoorsman and latter-day "mountain man." What makes Lilly's exploits so remarkable is that they were accomplished so late in his own and the region's history. He didn't arrive in the Southwest until Arizona and New Mexico were achieving statehood and he was in his mid-fifties. Nonetheless, the next twenty years saw Mr. Lilly's reputation as a lion and bear hunter *extraordinaire* increase to legendary proportions. He became one of the Southwest's best known characters. Although almost everyone who met him seemed compelled to write about him, it was J. Frank Dobie, the noted Texan author, who wrote the only comprehensive biography of Lilly. The following recollection in Ben's own words is included in *The Ben Lilly Legend,* originally published in 1950 by Curtis Publishing Company and recently reprinted by the University of Texas Press.

When he took on this grizzly on April 3, 1913, Ben Lilly was 58 years old. The U. S. Forest Service had employed Lilly to work on predatory animal control. Instead of concentrating on wolves, the preferred target of the Service, however, he continued his persecution of lions and bears. The result was mutual dissatisfaction between the independent mountaineer and early Forest Service administrators. Shortly afterwards, he went to work for the Predator and Rodent Control Branch of the U. S. Biological Survey—a more satisfactory assignment for all concerned.

Lilly was a dedicated (fanatic might be a better word) hunter of lions and bears. In fact, he was destroying the only world he knew. Possessed of great strength and endurance as well as an uncanny tracking ability, he, like others of his single-minded breed, had little love for the animals he knew so well. ✻

I struck this grizzly on Blue River and followed him for three days in snow. In places the snow had frozen and glazed over so that the bear did not make a visible track. In other places it was soft and waist deep. During the three days I did not have one mouthful to eat. I was wearing over my underclothes only a pair of blue cotton pants, a blue shirt and a light cotton sweater. I kept from freezing at night by building fires and sitting up by them.

Three times at very long ranges I shot this bear in the same hip while he was running from me. I had a slow-track dog tied to my waist. Once we came to a cave the bear had denned in the winter preceding. It was about eight feet wide and about sixteen feet back. At the mouth were six layers of black dirt between layers of snow, showing that the bear had dragged out earth that many times during the season of snowfall. This is just one instance of evidence that hibernating bears come out for short whiles during the winter. They will drink water while out but will not take a mouthful of food. Another grizzly I trailed in the Escalder [Escudilla] mountains in Arizona had made twelve trips in and out of his cave during his lay-up.

The wounded grizzly had left lots of fresh blood at his old den, but I knew it was not from any vital part. About three hundred yards east of the den I saw blood again, where the grizzly had scratched snow out of one of his summer beds and laid down. The trail worked on into thick spruce undergrowth. I looked to one side, getting ready to fire. Then right in front of my body, fifteen feet away, the bear popped out, charging me. My first shot hit him center in the breast; that checked him. My second shot was under the eye about three feet away. He fell against my side. I was bogged in snow waist-deep. I couldn't see the bear's head. He seemed to be drawing deep breaths. I fired another shot for his heart. I was wearing a knife eighteen inches long. I drove it for the heart. That finished him. It had been a test of endurance as well as a narrow escape.

I took careful measurements of this bear, according to government standards. He measured nine foot from the tip of his nose to the end of his tail; eight foot around the body. He stood five foot, eight inches high. His hind foot was twelve inches long and seven inches wide across the pad. On the top side, his claws were five inches long and at the base each of them was as wide as a man's finger. His ankles, both front and rear, measured fourteen inches around. His skull was eighteen inches long. There wasn't any way of weighing him. He was the largest bear and made the largest track of any I know of having been killed in the Rocky Mountains. I sent the skull and the hide to Washington.

After this bear died, I felt weak. My dogs and I both needed water. There was some under ice not far away, and we started to it. On the way we struck a lion track very fresh. I felt like a new man and took out in a run. The lion was soon treed and killed. We got water and went back to the grizzly bear. After I skinned him, the dogs and I had a good meal. I wrapped up in the skin by the carcass and slept as warm as if I were in a stove.

Hiring Ben Lilly
for the Biological Survey

J. Stokley Ligon

1916

Ben Lilly, one of the best Southwestern bear hunters, ranks with such luminaries as Jim Bridger and Kit Carson as one of the authentic folk figures of the American West. In this selection, taken from Elizabeth McFarland's 1974 *Wilderness of the Gila* (University of New Mexico Press), Ligon, one of the managers for the old Biological Survey (the precursor of the U. S. Fish and Wildlife Service), describes how he hired Lilly as a predator controller.

Lilly was born in Alabama in 1856, and, at an early age, showed an interest in trapping and hunting. In 1901 Lilly left his second wife and children for the wilds of northern Louisiana, where he became a market hunter. Five years later, after perfecting his hunting techniques for lions and bears, he left Louisiana for the Big Thicket region of Texas. In 1907 he guided President Theodore Roosevelt on a bear hunt there. The next year he moved west to hunt in northern Mexico, where he stayed until 1911, when he reentered the United States and began to hunt on behalf of ranches and for the government. He stayed in the Southwest until his death in 1936, working as a hunter and trapper.

Today Ben Lilly is remembered in the Gila country by a large bronze memorial marker on New Mexico highway 15 north of Pinos Altos. As Ligon reports, Lilly claimed to have killed "between two and three hundred" bears in his lifetime. If only a few of those that were grizzlies had lived, the situation for the grizzly in the Southwest might be very different today. 🐾

Through the Biological Survey field men, I knew of Ben Lilly while he was still in Louisiana. These field men went all over to contact biologists and men in wildlife work. One of them, Ned Hollister, found Ben Lilly hunting bear and mountain lions—or panthers as they call them in Louisiana. Hollister spent considerable time with Lilly and he would report his experiences back to the Biological Survey. From then on, the Biological Survey was in almost constant touch with Ben Lilly.

From Louisiana, Lilly went into south Texas, worked his way through there and on into Mexico. When the insurrection occurred in Mexico, it was pretty dangerous for men like Lilly to be hunting out in the wilds so he came out into southwestern New Mexico.

I already had considerable information about Ben Lilly, when I started predatory animal work in 1916 in the Gila Wilderness Area. From correspondence I had a pretty good idea what type of man he was, and I had talked to ranchers. He had been working on several ranches in western New Mexico. The rancher would agree to pay him so much bounty for each mountain lion, for an adult more than for a young one and the same way for a bear. He would confine his operations to that ranch while he was working for that man. He was so successful that most ranchers were glad to pay him bounty. He knew all the cow trails and bear trails and lion trails in that part of the country.

Dr. Fisher knew Lilly by reputation and was very much impressed with him and the work he was doing. He suggested that I see Lilly, so I got his address. He was on the Double Circle Ranch at that time, trapping or hunting mountain lions for bounty. I contacted him by letter and made a date to meet with him.

I crossed the range horseback from Chloride to the Double Circles. Lilly was camped at the Honeymoon Ranger Station on Eagle Creek. He had his dogs there at camp and was boiling mush for them when I got there. He was well supplied with hounds—I guess he had some of the best mountain lion hounds that have ever been in the state.

Ben Lilly was medium size, rather heavy for his height, and had a heavy beard. I'd say he was about 55 years old then (in 1916), and in his prime. He was very jolly and glad to see me, and very polite, as he always was in later visits also. Whenever he would see you coming, he would come to meet you. He was very liberal in his show of appreciation and was always wanting to do something for you, like cooking cornbread or fixing a meal.

He was a very unusual and likeable man—great for conversation on most any subject. He was especially well informed about the wild life of the country where he had worked. He had a fine memory and didn't seem to forget things that had transpired even in his young days in the Louisiana canebrakes. When President Theodore Roosevelt went to Louisiana on a bear hunt, he asked especially for Ben Lilly to go with him and they spent several days together. Lilly thought a great deal of the "Colonel."

To come back to my first meeting with Ben Lilly—I asked him if he would work for us in the Biological Survey. He was willing, but he wanted a salary of two hundred dollars a month. He could make that or more in bounty from ranchers. In fact, he said he preferred to work for so much a "piece," like a bounty. He said he felt there would be times that he didn't feel like getting out and working and doing his best. He was just conscientious enough that he wanted to put in every minute, and he felt that if he was working on his own time and just turning in animals, he would be more at ease.

The highest paid hunters we had in 1916 were starting in at a hundred and twenty-five dollars a month, so I told Mr. Lilly I would have to take it up with the officials in Washington and see if they would agree to that high a figure. He said at the time that he would guarantee to take four mountain lions a month for that salary. He said he did not want to work for the Survey.

Finally Dr. Nelson, who was in charge at that time, consented to pay Ben Lilly two hundred dollars a month, and he was employed just for hunting lion and big bear. He did make good and it was quite a satisfaction to have him working for us.

He could deliver on an average of four mountain lions a month, sometimes he would get more and sometimes less, depending on the conditions of the section where he hunted. I think all together he killed between two and three hundred mountain lions in New Mexico, including the ones for bounty paid by the ranchers.

Ben Lilly kept a diary with a rather accurate account of his activities. He wrote a very pretty hand. He said he had diaries and camp equipment cached all over at different places, because he went afoot and couldn't carry things. He would make an accumulation at one place and then leave it there and go on and accumulate things at another place. I understand they found a rather important diary at the GOS Ranch, but it was in an old shack and the rats had gotten to it and rain, too, so it was illegible.

Mr. Culberson was in charge of the GOS Ranch and he thought a lot of Ben Lilly. When the American Livestock Association had a meeting in El Paso, Mr. Culberson brought Ben Lilly to the meeting and Lilly made them a speech regarding hunting mountain lion and bear. Some of the other hunters claimed that Lilly was telling a tall tale when he said in that speech he had killed four hundred bears. But if Ben Lilly said he had killed that many, then that is how many he killed! He was always perfectly honest.

Along the latter part of his years, he told me he knew the total of how many lions and how many bear he had killed, but he only told the Biological Survey how many he killed in New Mexico and Arizona. I think in New Mexico it was between two and three hundred mountain lion and about as many bear.

Some people claim he didn't kill many bear but I know definitely that he did. While he was working for us, I have been with him and trailed him in the mountains on foot following his dogs many days and often spent nights with him, and I have known of many bear he killed. It was no trouble for Lilly to kill a bear. If they would tell him there was a bear in a locality, he would take his dogs and he would be in there a few days and come out with a bear hide.

Ben Lilly was very modest, and if Montague Stevens or somebody like that dominated the conversation on hunting bear, Lilly would just go into his shell and let them talk. He told me once, "Why, if I

would tell them how many I have killed in all of my experience in all
my life, people just wouldn't believe it." So he never told them. Ben
Lilly had killed bear from the time he was a very young man in the
canebrakes and bottoms of Mississippi and Louisiana, then clear
through to Mexico and Arizona, and finally New Mexico where he
died near the wilderness he knew so well.

Hunting Stock-Killing Grizzlies

Jack Tooker

ca. 1920

This popularized story by a free-lance ranch-hand and predator trapper appeared in 1949 in *Roundup of Western Literature,* edited by Oren Arnold and published by Banks Upshaw and Co. of Dallas. In it Tooker relates how he eliminated not only a stock-killing problem, but what may have been the last reproducing population of grizzlies from the Sycamore Canyon region of west-central Arizona. The last grizzly of record from this area was a big male killed in 1922 by Ramsey Patterson and Jimmy Norman in nearby Government Canyon (see D. Brown, *The Grizzly in the Southwest,* University of Oklahoma Press, 1985). The present Sycamore Canyon Wilderness Area and the canyons to the west remain great bear country and worthy of consideration as a future grizzly reintroduction site.

What makes this tale especially interesting is that it documents the great amount of money, effort, and risk expended to remove grizzlies from their final "holdouts." Obviously, the depredations of even a few grizzlies were intolerable given pervasive livestock grazing in brushy, remote areas during periods of food scarcity. Even the heightened awareness of experienced grizzlies was insufficient to protect them from determined men who knew the bear's natural history and habits. Nor did the remorse expressed by these men on killing these magnificent animals overcome the rationale that there was no choice but to eliminate these "outlaws." 🌿

This story goes back twenty-odd years. It was April. The bears were out. Grizzlies were killing stock on both sides of the Sycamore Canyon. The D. K. cow outfit controlled all the range on the east side of the Sycamore from the Santa Fe Railroad to the Verde River, and the Bar Cross outfit had the same claim to the west side.

Tom Wagner was part owner and in charge of the Bar Cross outfit. He had a pack of hounds and kept the bears stirred up, occasionally killing a black bear, but with no grizzlies to his credit. The dogs just could not stop the grizzlies. They would not tree or stand at bay as black bears do, but would shake off or kill their tormentors and keep going down into the roughest part of the canyon, where even a dog could not follow.

The cowmen were of the opinion that the country was full of stock-killing grizzlies, but after a survey of the country and studying the bear signs I informed them that, in my opinion, two bears were doing most of the killing, and that they were perhaps, mates with cubs.[1] The cowmen had organized several ineffectual hunts for the bears, always in hopes that they would be fortunate enough not to meet up with any of the bruin family; and in this they had been successful, never having bagged bears of any variety.

The acorn crop of the previous year had been sparse and, added to that, the snow was staying on much later than usual this spring, which made a combination of reasons why the bears were driven to seek an exclusive diet of beef.

The killing was becoming so wanton, the stockmen decided to offer a reward for skins. The figures agreed upon were $1100 for the two bears—$700 for the male and $400 for his mate. They made the usual mistake of believing that the male was the worst offender and doing most of the killing, whereas the female grizzly is by far the more destructive and dangerous, especially if she has cubs.

Prior to this time I had killed nine grizzlies, and considered it the

[1]Now known to be an erroneous interpretation.—Eds.

most adventurous sport I had ever experienced. So, with the thrills of a grizzly hunt in my mind, and the added attraction of $1100, I let it be known that I would try for the reward. I had known of several cases where stockmen had offered rewards for the pelts of certain cattle-destroying animals, but when the skins were produced the rewards had failed to materialize.

I knew this particular hunt would be hazardous—especially since it looked like I would make it alone—so, in order to insure my receiving the $1100 in case the hunt proved a success, as I hoped it would, I rode out to the ranch house to talk it over with Tom.

While riding through the canyon Tom had come across the big bear on two different occasions; just a glimpse of him each time, but enough to see that he was what is commonly called a bald-faced grizzly—having a white stripe on his forehead. Regardless of whether I killed this particular bear, Tom assured me that the money would be mine if I produced grizzly skins.

"This offer stands," he said. "A big skin gets the $700 and a small one $400. . . . Boys"—turning to some of the riders who were sitting around the little shack that served as an office—"you were witness to what I have just told Jack." Turning to me, he asked, "Is that all right?"

"Sure," I said. "I just wanted to be sure of some kind of an understanding."

"Well, kid," he drawled out, "you may get the bears and you may not; but if you're goin' down in the canyon to hunt for them, you better take someone with you. It's a durn fool notion to go alone, an' you ain't got no business to do it."

I informed him that I had been trying for a week to get someone to go with me and had offered to split the money fifty-fifty.

"And that offer still stands, boys," I said to the cowboys, but none of them felt the urge for bear hunting at that time.

However, they were all interested in my plans for the trip, although they informed me in no uncertain terms just how foolish they thought I was to undertake the trip alone, and all the more so after I began unfolding to them just how I planned to engineer the adventure.

I had decided I would start the hunt in Tully Canyon. Tom agreed that was about the best shot, as the bears generally came up Tully Canyon. My plan was to go down into the canyon on foot, locate where the bears were doing their killing, and catch them in the act, if possible. If I had no luck in that, and the snow stayed on, I could at least track them to their dens and kill them there.

"Well, kid," Tom drawled, "maybe that's the right way to go at it, but you're sure takin' plenty chances. Better take a hoss and stop at our lower cabin. The bears have been workin' near there, and I'd not feel so uneasy 'bout you if I knew you had a hoss and a cabin for sort o' headquarters."

I argued that no one had killed a grizzly in several years, using that method, and I wanted to try my luck with my own scheme. All I intended to take with me was a sleeping bag I had rigged up myself, two extra pairs of heavy wool socks, my gun, .33 rifle, two boxes of cartridges, and grub enough to last about ten days.

The more I discussed the trip and my plans with the boys, the more eager I became to start out as soon as possible.

Tom mentioned that they were going out with the chuck wagon to one of the camps near the mouth of the canyon the next morning, and I decided to go that far with them.

In spite of my excitement, I slept well and got up bright and early the next morning, eager to be off. For several miles after leaving the ranch, the wagon tires had sung us a merry song on the frost-crusted snow, but now it had warmed up, with splendid prospects for more snow. Arriving at the Bar Cross cabin at about two in the afternoon, we unhitched the team. I put the horses in the barn, unharnessed and fed them, while Tom started a fire in the cabin stove. While Tom got dinner, I carried the stuff out of the wagon, got my own things together, went into the storeroom and packed up enough chuck to last me for ten days—plenty of bacon, as I knew I could always get fresh meat; and the rest of the supplies were the very lightest possible.

Pretty soon Tom called, "Come and get it, or I'll throw it out to the dogs!"

I yelled right back, "Coming!"

While we each got on the outside of a big steak, we talked of my trip. Those steaks were from a fat yearling and had been frozen for a month or more. They were simply wonderful, and so were all the trimmings—biscuits, spuds, and so on—and Tom could sure make biscuits. I was eating what I thought was my last meal under a roof for ten days or more (at least). But Tom had another thought, and it beat mine all hollow.

He asked, "When you startin', kid?"

"Just as soon as I get through with this steak."

"No," he says, "you get a good night's rest and get the reports from the cowboys when they come in, and when I turn you loose tomorrow you'll have most of the day before you. Why, goldurn it, if I was to take you down there this evening, it would be dark before you could find a place to hole up for the night."

"Well, Tom, if you're worrying about me, just cut that out. I'll be all right. I'll get a bear, and maybe two, if my grub holds out, and I'll be back."

"Well, kid," he comes back, "I'm not worryin' none, but I am goin' to leave you a hoss in the stable at the J. D. ranch. That's the nearest ranch to the Sycamore Canyon, and I'll leave you some grub in the house in a big can, so the rats won't get it. One of the boys can go by every day to feed and water the horse. You can make it to the J. D. ranch from the east rim of the Sycamore in about one day, if you run out of supplies; and I'm guessing that if you kill any bears, that's where you will get them. There ain't been much killing on this side lately. But I saw the D. K. foreman last night, and he said that the bear was just raisin' hell over there."

The cowboys soon came in from different directions and reported having seen no bears, fresh bear signs or kills. It began snowing about dark. That was ideal and the very thing I had hoped for. All bear signs would be fresh and would make my work easier. It was still snowing in the morning.

After breakfast we saddled our horses and left the ranch in about eight inches of fresh snow. There was not so much snow lower down, and at Tully Canyon only about three or four inches. We rode down the north rim of Tully Canyon to the rim of the Sycamore, and there Tom left me, wishing me luck.

I adjusted my pack, which weighed about forty pounds, gun and all. I had good shoepacks. I worked along the rim of the Sycamore for about four miles, almost opposite the J. D. ranch and straight across the canyon from the D. K. winter camp. I had seen several lion tracks but no bear sign; so decided to cross the canyon. It had stopped snowing when I reached the bottom of the Sycamore. The brush thickets were wet and the rocks slippery. The Sycamore Canyon is a miniature Grand Canyon, highly colored, rough and rugged. Many cliff dwellings, sealed caves and ruins bear testimony that it was inhabited long before Columbus discovered America.

By the time I had crossed the bottom of the canyon, which is wide at this point, I was hungry and tired. So I built a fire, broiled a steak, made coffee, warmed up some of Tom's biscuits, and enjoyed a feed fit for a king.

As I had hoped, there were bear signs in the bottom of the canyon. They had their trails. In some places these trails were just tunnels through the thickets of brush and undergrowth. But none of the signs seen so far were made by the species I was in search of—namely, the ponderous grizzly.

After a little rest, I started to climb out of the canyon and reached the D. K. winter cabin before dark. I was in fairly deep snow again. There were no man or horse tracks, so I knew there had been no one about since the fresh snow had fallen. I found the cabin well supplied with firewood, so I soon had a fire roaring in the stove and began preparations for supper. As soon as it got dark, the skunks and rats appeared and began to play about the floor. Fortunately for me, the cabin contained an old bed, so I was able to sleep up off the floor and somewhat out of their line of play, but even at that, either rats or skunks, or perhaps both, ran over me frequently during the night.

I managed to fall asleep at intervals, for I was very weary. I would wake up with a start to hear the tap-tapping of the skunks' feet on the floor. They were absolutely safe as far as my molesting them was concerned. I was willing to give them the full run of the place and, sensing my indifference to them, they repaid me by refraining from loosing the vicious odor that has made them such a despised and much-to-be-avoided animal. Added to the discomfiture caused by the rodents, the shack was cold and before morning I froze out. I got up and built a fire, and as soon as it was light enough to see, I prepared a hearty breakfast.

The D. K. people kept a large box of food supplies in the cabin. The box was well lined with tin and kept the rodents out. I used the D. K. supplies as much as possible for my breakfast, saving my own, for I knew that upon those supplies depended to a very great measure my success or failure.

After breakfast I left the cabin, going south on the west side of Buck Ridge, crossing the heads of many little canyons that ran off into the Sycamore. I had travelled until about ten o'clock and was west of Turkey Butte and the old, historic Mooney Trail, when, on crossing the head of a canyon, I came upon two fresh tracks. The one was made by a very large bear and the other, though large, was smaller than the big one.

I was growing tired, although I had not covered much ground, but when I saw those bear tracks and the immensity of them, I forgot everything but the thrill of the hunt ahead of me. The tracks had been made the night before and were going straight south. After following them for about two hours, I came to the mouth of a small canyon, where the tracks separated. The big fellow had gone straight down into the main canyon that empties into the Sycamore, while the smaller tracks led up a little side canyon. This situation meant a den and cubs to me, but I wanted to be sure. The little canyon was full of rocks and oaks of all sizes. As the wind was blowing from the south, I climbed out on the north side. I did not want the old girl to wind me, for if she had a den and cubs I could get her and the cubs any time I wanted them, but it was through her that I hoped to trap the old daddy bear.

After getting on top, I could see that the canyon came to an end in less than half a mile. Also, that it was a box canyon all the way, and narrow. No animal—not even a bear—could scale its walls. I went the full length of the canyon, keeping away from the rim so as not to be seen, but frequently I would slip up and peer carefully over to see if the tracks were still there. At the end of the canyon the tracks went into a cave. I could see back under the shelf and into the cave a short distance, but could see or hear nothing. Yet I was satisfied that the cave housed a mother grizzly and her cubs.

I spent the rest of the day in locating a place to camp. I chose a cave in a small canyon less than a mile west of the den, rustled enough dry wood for my stay, then gathered pine needles and boughs for my bed. I had selected a cave without any small holes in the end, so as to be sure that I was not living in a rat or skunk den. As this cave was to be my home for several days, I made everything as comfortable as possible with my limited supplies and equipment. Time seemed literally to fly. It was dark before I had supper over and a small lunch put up for the morrow. Since I had made my bed well back and had a good fire in the mouth of the cave, I slept warm and very comfortably. In fact, my sleeping quarters were luxurious in comparison to my experience of the previous night.

I was up at the break of day and immediately walked to the mouth of the canyon, in hopes that I might catch the two bears coming in from their night's hunt. But I was too late. According to the tracks, they had been there just a few moments before I had arrived. They had come in from a different direction this time. The smaller track had led up the same side canyon as before, but the big one took off in a new direction, and I decided to follow. What a merry chase he led me—over the roughest part of that rough country, and at last wound up in the bottom of Sycamore Canyon, in dense thickets and with no snow for tracking.

I decided I would have to give up the hunt for that morning, and was thinking with no pleasure of the tiresome walk back, when I came to an unexpected clearing. Looking across the clearing, I observed a large animal about one hundred yards distant, in the edge of the thicket. It was looking at me and I was vaguely conscious that it had a white stripe in the face. A few cattle, in search of food, had got into the bottom from the east side, so I thought the animal merely a cow. And then it moved, and how quickly I knew it was not a cow but rather the object of my hunt. I was not ready for a shot, and before I could sight he was into cover. I saw him no more that day. A bear is no fool, and I was satisfied they knew I was in their country. They doubtless had crossed my tracks many times.

I gave up, for the time being, the idea of catching them at the mouth of the den canyon and decided, instead, to locate the place where they were doing their killing. I found that they had no regular place to kill. They met each night at a different place. They would each go straight to the meeting point; then hunt together. They picked the roughest places where the stock were ranging. I found partly eaten cattle with broken hips, broken-down backs, sides caved in, and broken necks, showing that these grizzlies had no regular method of killing, as the lion does. In one small canyon I found enough bones to fill a box car—all the results of bear killings.

After they had killed and gorged to their satisfaction, Mr. Bear would escort his mate to the mouth of the canyon where the den was located. But when they reached the mouth of the canyon, that was as far as he was allowed to go. According to the tracks in the snow, they had evidently had quite an argument one morning, and I rather suspect that he wanted to go and take a look at the children. But no large bear tracks led up that canyon, so I concluded that Mrs. Bear had upheld her feminine prerogative of deciding what was to be done, and Father Bear had gone on his way without a visit to the children.

Perhaps you are thinking: "What a simple matter to catch those bears at the mouth of the little canyon!"

True, it would have been, except for the fact that all their movements were made under cover of darkness. It is hazardous enough to meet one grizzly bear in good light, where your sights are plain, but to meet two of them in the dark, and one of them a mother, with cubs near—well, that would be recorded as a plain case of suicide.

I spent six nights in my little cave, and five mornings found me at the mouth of that little canyon at daybreak, but always I was just a little late. We had little squalls of snow almost every day and I spent most of the daylight hours trying to track down or locate the male bear. But my efforts bore me no success. He led me in different directions and to different places each time. Once he took me down the Mooney Trail four or five miles, and still another time he took me to the very bottom of Secret Canyon. How cleverly he managed always to elude me!

My supplies were getting low and I was growing discouraged. I decided to try once more to catch them at the entrance of the den canyon.

It was still dark that early April morning when I took my stand. I had barely settled down to wait when two dark objects came lumbering down the main canyon. They looked larger in the shadows than they actually were. I could discern them plainly enough, locating their heads, bodies and limbs, but although I tried again and again, I was unable to see my sights.

My impulse was to fire regardless, but my experience told me that a wounded grizzly, even in good light, is one of the most dangerous assailants on earth; so I forebore my impulse and contented myself with watching them.

The bears parted as usual—the mother hastening to her cubs and the old male going back the way he had come. I knew it was useless to attempt to track him in that shadowy light, so I rested where I was until the sun lighted the eastern sky. Then, following the same route I had taken when I located the female's den, I went directly to the cave, staying well upon the rim.

As I neared the cave, I could hear the cubs. They must have been quarreling over their breakfast. Several times a chubby little fellow wabbled to the mouth of the den, and at last the mother herself stuck her head out. I was almost straight above her, close enough that I could see her eyes. I moved slightly until I could sight just a little back of her eyes, and then attempted to place a bullet. I was over-cautious about striking the shelf rock and did not hold fine enough. The bullet struck her between the eyes, missing the brain. Out she charged like a mad bull, tearing oak brush down, looking everywhere for me. She could not see me, and the wind was favorable, so that she could not smell me.

In her mad charge she went tearing out of sight down the little canyon. In a brief time she came slipping back, stopping every few feet to listen. As she came under my stand I placed a bullet just back of the hump. It ranged down, passing through her heart and tearing it to shreds. She died trying to locate the enemy. I went back down into the canyon and came up to the mouth of the cave where she lay. The cave was shallow and in the very back end were three grizzly cubs. They were about the size of small shepherd dogs. Each cub had a white stripe on his face and a small white cross on the breast, all three being marked like their daddy. I tried to make friends with them, but they fought and scratched like wild cats.

After skinning out the mother bear, I killed two of the cubs and tied up the other one. I wanted to carry him to my cave and take him to town alive. But even with all feet tied he would not cease fighting. It was a hopeless task to carry that biting, fighting, scratching cub, so I was forced to shoot him and skin him, along with his brother and sister.

Taking the large grizzly skin and my bed, I made the D. K. winter cabin early that afternoon, and, much to my surprise and pleasure, found Curly Grey, who had come in the day before with a pack horse and supplies. He was glad of my success and encouraged me to remain longer and try again for the big fellow. He helped me pack more supplies over to my cave and took the three small bear-skins back to the ranch with him.

I was very anxious to know what the old bear had done when the mother bear failed to come and meet him, and so I was at the mouth of Bear Canyon at daybreak. He had been there, and when the mother failed to show up, he had gone up to the little canyon to investigate. His tracks showed that he was still there. To follow him would be foolish, besides being very dangerous. The brush was so thick that it would be very difficult to get in an effective shot. Therefore, I decided on a stand on the north side of the canyon, above and about one hundred yards from where he must come out. I had gone only half the distance when I heard the brush cracking. He had come out into the opening, and such a wonderful specimen he was!

As he came to my tracks he stopped short, looking everywhere for me; then he stood on his hind feet, peering at every angle. At last he located me. He stared straight in my direction for several minutes, but as I made not the slightest move, he shifted his gaze. I was filled with admiration for that majestic animal. I would not have killed the mother and cubs but for the fact that they were outlaws, stock killers, with a bounty on their heads. But with this fellow there was no choice.

Doubtless he reasoned that I was responsible for the disappearance of his family, and, in all probability, would have trailed me down, for he showed no fear. The hair stood up all over his body; he was ready for battle.

He stood less than fifty yards from me. A body shot at that distance is very dangerous, as a grizzly shot directly through the heart will live long enough to go one hundred yards and kill ten men, should that many be in his path.

As he turned his head to one side, I drew a bead just back of his ear, hoping to break his neck, and pressed the trigger. He fell like a beef.

Believing him dead, I jumped from my hiding place. But the bullet had only creased him. He revived as quickly as he had passed out. As he raised up I had no chance for a head or neck shot, but took a quick side shot for the heart. He charged with surprising speed.

I pumped my four remaining bullets into him in rapid succession.

Any one of the wounds inflicted would have caused death in time, but now his body seemed impervious to them. With a half ton of angry bear charging, time flies, one thinks quickly. Those beady eyes were two balls of fire, his mouth was open and the bloody froth flowing freely. An awful sight to behold, especially in a lonely canyon miles from help.

Slipping a cartridge into the empty chamber of my gun, I held my fire. He had reared up on his hind legs less than ten feet from me. As he lurched forward I thrust the muzzle of my rifle at his open mouth, intending to pull the gun off and then use it for a club as a last resort. But with a single stroke of his huge gray paw, he slapped the gun from my hand as easily as though he were merely brushing away an annoying insect. My finger was inside the trigger guard, and the jerk discharged the gun, the bullet going wild. The gun was cast aside. He struck at my head; I ducked. Another swing that was so close I felt the wind. He closed in; I ducked under his massive arms. Then something happened—it seemed as if a mighty pile driver had plunged down upon my head, forcing, driving it down between my shoulders.

Late that afternoon I regained consciousness. The dead grizzly was lying on my left leg; my right was broken. I had lain in the slushy snow and was wet and cold. It seemed that every bone in my body was broken or crushed. I made several ineffectual attempts to sit up before I finally attained a sitting posture. But it was worth all the effort it cost, for it probably saved my life.

A most welcome sight met my eyes. I had told Curly that I would be back to the cabin for breakfast by ten o'clock. When I did not show up by noon, he had started in search of me. He had tracked me to that point. When I sat up, the movement had attracted the horse's attention; Curly saw me and came on the run. He rolled the bear off my leg with the aid of a rope attached to the bear's paw and the horn of the saddle.

I must have been a gruesome sight—soaked from head to foot with bloody froth. It took all the nerve I could muster and Curly's help to get me into the saddle. It seemed at times that I could not endure for another moment that long and excruciating three-mile trip to the D. K. winter cabin. After what seemed an eternity, we reached the cabin and Curly put me to bed. He cut my clothes off and bathed and dressed my many wounds as best he could.

After setting an old can filled with water near my bed, he left me, to ride to the Garland ranger station at the head of Sycamore Canyon to phone Doctor Mitchell. The doctor caught No. 8, Atchison, Topeka and Santa Fe train and got off at a station called Maine, where Curly met him with a saddle horse.

I was conscious most of the time Curly was gone, but fully expected to be dead and half of my body devoured by skunks and rats before he returned. It would be impossible to describe the inferno they created for me. They ran over my body, across my face, ate holes in my bloody clothes, and made a meal of my boot tops. The only movement I could make was to turn my head slightly from side to side, but that was so painful that the torture of rats and skunks was preferable.

About daylight Curly and the doctor came in, having made the trip down the east side of the Sycamore—some twenty-seven miles—in about seven hours, which was fast time considering the nature of the country and the snow. After setting the leg and dressing my wounds, they left to examine the bear and skin it. One bullet had torn away part of his heart—no doubt the second shot. He was literally all shot up inside.

When they returned with the bearskin, they asked innumerable questions about how it happened. I told them as best I could, up until the time the bear hit me. I could not tell how long he had lived. I only knew he had lived long enough almost to succeed in finishing me.

Those six weeks I was forced to spend in that rat-and-skunk-infested D. K. winter cabin, while waiting for my leg to mend and my wounds to heal, left memories that can never be erased from my mind. The rats never bit me and the skunks made no odor. Why should they when they had their own way and were not molested? I was forced to invent many time-killing devices to fill in the lonely hours I spent while Curly was out looking after cattle. Before I was able to depart I had most of the skunks named, and prided myself on being able to recognize them at sight.

One of the greatest joys I have ever known was when the doctor pronounced my leg as being in such a condition that I could be moved and could leave the cabin that had housed rats, skunks, and myself for six long, fiendish weeks. My wounds healed in due time and I regained perfect health, but at times, when going back in retrospection, I can again feel the effects of the terrible mauling I received at the hands of old Father Grizzly.

Old Man Grizzly

G. W. Evans

1930

G. W. "Dub" Evans was one of those transplanted Texas ranchmen who maintained a pack of hounds and spent about as much time hunting bears and lions as ranching. Although he later grew to value these animals, he maintained a lifelong hatred for wolves and was not satisfied until government hunters trapped the last wolf in his theatre of operations southwest of Magdalena, New Mexico. Evans, in fact, had a close relationship with personnel of the U. S. Biological Survey, as not only was the skull of the grizzly in this account sent to the National Museum, but records of that institution list another grizzly attributed to him from Magdalena Baldy. Evans thus took, or knew of, the last recorded grizzlies from New Mexico.

"Old Man Grizzly" is a chapter in Evans's book of recollections of his hunting adventures—*Slash Ranch Hounds,* published in 1951 by the University of New Mexico Press. The hunt takes place in April 1930, in New Mexico's Black Range near the head of the Mimbres River. Present with Evans on the eight-day hunt were his brother Lee, Bud McGahey of Borger, Texas, and A. L. Inman, on whose Healy Ranch the hunt took place. The kill was near Hillsboro Peak; the skin of the bear hangs on a wall at the Evans Ranch headquarters (now the Montrose Cattle Company) where G. W. Evans, Jr., graciously allowed me to look at it in 1984.

That all bears were protected in New Mexico at the time of the hunt was no problem. The law required only that a permit be obtained for taking stock killers—an easy feat for Evans who was highly respected by state wildlife officers as well as by federal trappers. It also appears to have mattered little whether the permit was secured before or after the depredation, or before or after the bear was brought to justice. It is informative that it never occurred to Evans that grizzlies might henceforth be forever absent from the Black Range.

Evans's writings display the Southwesterner's ambivalent attitude toward wildlife. The sympathetic response to wounded deer, antelope, and livestock expressed by ranchers is diagnostic of their emotional concern for animals. The implied cruelty of a mountain lion kill, the savage and wanton destruction by depredating wolves, and the cumbersome attacks by stock-killing bears violate the sensibilities of those engaged in animal husbandry. Such carnage justifies almost any effort to get rid of these "killers." Therein lies much of the rural community's antagonism against predators. It is a cultural attribute that must be considered if bears and other large carnivores are to be preserved. 🕸

We moved from the ranch to the head of Black Canyon, taking two days to make the trip. We left the hounds tied up the first day, taking only one along to look for signs. We found a grizzly track headed north about six miles from camp on the east side of the range. I took the hounds the next day and was to go down into the rough country where we saw the track. The other men took stands out on top at places where they thought the bear would come out if we got a start. The track we found the day before seemed to be old, but the hounds finally took it. They trailed it into a rough canyon about half a mile north and hit a red-hot trail. I had about twenty hounds, most of them young. They had not been hunted with lately and were fresh and eager to run anything. Just as they went off under the first rim of this rough canyon, they hit the fresh trail of the bear where he came from a cow that he had killed about a half mile down the canyon just east of where I was. All the hounds except Little Brownie and one other took the back end of the trail that led down to the kill. I ran out to the edge of the bluff to listen, and heard Little Brownie and the other hound barking "bayed" right down under me. They had already come up on the bear and were not a hundred yards from me. The brush was so thick I could not see the bear at all. I waited there a few minutes and could hear him breaking the brush as he walked around with the hounds barking at him.

There were a lot of bluffs there just over the bear and it sounded to me as though he was coming up the hill and was going to pass west of me. I moved a few hundred yards west and when I got where I could listen I found the bear had run east and right under where I had moved from. All the hounds that had gone on the back trail were out of hearing. I found later that after they had reached the kill, they had scattered and were running deer and coyotes. The last time I heard Little Brownie, he was still baying the bear and going southeast exactly away from where the men were stationed. They never did know what happened. It was too rough to ride so I followed Little Brownie on foot and could see this big old bear track every once in a while. I finally lost the track, and the wind came up, so I lost out entirely.

I hunted Little Brownie all afternoon. I went back to my horse and made a big circle but did not find anything. Hounds began to come to me, but no Little Brownie. I went back to camp late that evening, with most of the hounds, and Little Brownie came in about ten o'clock.

While in the canyon where the cow was killed, I saw the track of another fair-sized bear. Three of Lee's hounds didn't come in, so, next day, Lee and A. L. Inman went to the Ladder Ranch to look for them, and the rest of us moved camp about five miles south and camped in the saddle between the head of Mimbres and Palomas creeks, right on top of the Continental Divide. We had a pretty camp and a good place for our horses. Lee and A.L. Inman found Lee's hounds at the Ladder Ranch and got back to our new camp late that evening.

The next day, we all decided to go down near the kill. I was to take Little Brownie and go down to the cow and get the trail straightened out. When I got down near the kill, Little Brownie struck a trail and I soon found that it was the little bear instead of the grizzly. The grizzly hadn't come back. Lee and A. L. Inman let the other hounds go when they heard Little Brownie, but it was a big, rough country and before they could get to him he had gone into a rough canyon behind a point and neither the men nor the hounds could hear him.

McGahey and Deming Inman had taken a stand at the head of the canyon that Little Brownie was going up. Most of the hounds that Lee and A. L. Inman had released had run off after a deer and were scattered all over the country, most of them going in the opposite direction to the bear. The bear came out in sight of Bud and Deming Inman and they shot at him about fifteen times. We all got together about where the shooting occurred and saw Little Brownie go out by himself where the bear had gone. A. L. Inman and I waited there to gather up the hounds and put them on the trail as soon as they came back to us. The other boys went out on top to work around to some deep saddles on top of the divide in the direction the bear was going. We waited there about an hour and finally gathered up eleven hounds. We had to go around the head of a rough canyon to get to the bear's trail. As soon as we got over there the hounds hit the trail and left in "high." We followed them but they crossed a rough canyon or two and left us far behind. We went on in their direction though, and found them treed in about the third canyon and only about a mile east of our camp. We killed the bear, a brown male, and as Lee and the other boys were within hearing distance, we all soon got together. I guess Little Brownie already had the bear treed before the other hounds got there, or the bear would have been much farther off after having been shot at so many times.

The next morning we started south from camp and hadn't gone a mile until Little Brownie struck a trail, and we saw from the tracks that it was the old big grizzly, going south right down the Government trail. He went down the trail for about six miles, all of the hounds trailing. It was all we could do to stay within hearing, loping nearly all the time. They finally turned off east and followed near the main divide for about two miles, when they went off into the head of a very rough canyon and we heard them come up on the bear. Grizzlies don't run when the hounds come up on them.

All six of us were together on this rough point and we decided that

Bud and I would go on foot, as it was too rough to ride, and see if we could get a shot at the bear. There were eight or ten hounds down there making a lot of noise. The brush was so thick one could see only a few yards ahead. The bear didn't stay there very long, but I think we got within fifty or a hundred yards of him before he ran. As soon as he ran, the hounds overtook him again and he must have turned on them, for all but Little Brownie and possibly one or two others came back in a bunch to me. I hurried to the edge of a big point that they had gone over and when I got where I could look out I heard Little Brownie off on a mountainside, and located him and the big bear going around the side of the mountain. Little Brownie was only a few feet from the bear's heels, and the bear was in a lope. There was only one other hound behind Little Brownie, a black hound, either In- man's Dobie, or Lee's Black Alice. The bear was headed south or southeast and going off into the north fork of the Animas.

It began to get pretty hot and I thought the bear might stop when he crossed the canyon, as there were lots of big bluffs there, with thick brush and a running stream of water. I hurried off the mountain thinking I would get a shot at the bear as he crossed the canyon. Bud and I had gotten separated in the first canyon the hounds had crossed. There were some big falls in the canyon and as Little Brownie was the only hound barking I soon lost hearing of him when I got near the water.

There were eleven hounds with me at this time, none of them trying to follow the bear. I did not know what had become of Little Brownie except that I knew he had quit or had crossed the canyon out of hearing. As he didn't show up, I figured he was still with the bear, so I sized up the country and picked out a saddle on the south side of the canyon that would be a likely place for the bear to come out. I climbed up to this saddle and found where the old bear had gone through, with Little Brownie's tracks right in his. The other hounds took up the trail there and followed it as it began to turn west and into still rougher country. As soon as I got well over onto the rim of the next canyon, I could hear Little Brownie baying about a mile west of me. A few of the hounds went to him, but most of them came back. I could not get to him without crossing a country where I believed the bear could hear me, so I decided I would go off into the canyon and up to a point where I could climb out and come up on the bear from the opposite side. It took me about an hour to do this, and when I came up over the point where I thought the bear was, he had moved, but I was within about a hundred yards of him.

Several of the hounds went over to where he was but they didn't stay long. The brush was so thick I could not see the bear, although I was close and could tell where he was by the hounds. He kept moving, staying in one place for only a few minutes. It was about noon and getting awfully hot. I kept climbing around after the hounds and the bear, and I was so close to them the hounds with me would go to him every once in a while but would not stay long.

The wind began to blow, and there were several minutes that I could not hear the hounds at all. I kept hunting around and could see the old bear's tracks. I knew he was giving out or was too hot to travel, and he seemed determined not to leave this mountain. It was about the roughest place in the country, with the brush so thick I could hardly crowd through it. I sat down on a rock at the edge of a point to rest, and had been there only a few minutes when I heard the hounds just below me. I moved over a little farther and could hear them plainly, only a short distance below me. I got down there a few minutes later, and there were three hounds with the bear this time— Black Alice, Dobie, and Little Brownie. As I came near, some of the other hounds went to them and began barking at the bear.

I slipped down towards them and kept getting closer. I could only see for a few feet because of the thick brush, but finally located the bear. He was lying down with his right side to me and I could see he was panting. When I was about fifteen or twenty feet from him, I shot at about where I thought his shoulder was, or a little behind. He made an awful noise and began to break the brush and bellow like a bull. I got a little closer and could see he was staggering badly. I shot him again in the neck and he died a few seconds later.

He was on a steep hillside but the brush was so thick he rolled only about thirty feet, breaking the brush as he rolled over it. Not a hound bit him, even after he was dead. I never saw such a bear as he was. I caught hold of a foot and could not turn him over.

I knew that if I did not get help the hide would be wasted, so I left the bear and went to a high point and shot three times. I sure was pleased when Lee answered me with answering shots. Lee finally got to within about three hundred yards of where I was, and we began to talk to each other and decided what to do about getting the hide out.

We decided to get Lee's horse as close to the bear as we could, skin the bear, and bring the skin out on the horse. We got back to the bear at three o'clock and got him skinned by five. We got the skin back to the horse and then worked our way off into the canyon where there was water, and there we stayed until morning. Then we loaded the skin and began to climb out toward the top of the mountain where we had left the boys and horses the day before. Lee walked and led his horse all the way out, but the huge skin was so heavy that the horse gave out carrying the load. If we had not had a horse near the scene of the kill we never could have gotten the skin out at all.

We got out on top about ten o'clock and the boys met us with some food and fresh horses. We got the skin to camp about three o'clock. When we went the next day to get some pictures of the bear's carcass we found that there was another grizzly on the same mountainside and found where the other bear had gone out. We decided, however, that, as our horses were pretty well tired out and our grain supply running low, we would pack up and move out toward home instead of sending for grain to continue the hunt.

The "little" bear were getting so thick that we could not go in any direction without striking a trail. When we moved out of camp we led Little Brownie to keep him off bear trails. He struck a trail even wearing a collar and chain.

A Yarn and True Stories
Nat Straw Told

J. Frank Dobie

ca. 1930s

The writings of J. Frank Dobie are well known to students of the Southwest, reflecting the author's varied skills as regional historian, folklorist, chronicler, and storyteller. Dobie made a life-long commitment to interpreting the rich oral traditions of his native Texas and of Mexico. In this selection, which first appeared in *Vanity Fair* in 1931 and was reprinted in Elizabeth McFarland's *Wilderness of the Gila* (University of New Mexico Press, 1974), Straw tells of his pet grizzly bear Geronimo. Straw's yarn belongs to the rich frontier tradition of exaggerated heroic narratives. Although Nat Straw undoubtedly possessed great skills as a trapper and naturalist, it is for his ability as a storyteller that he is best known.[1] ✿

Nat Straw led all the rest in an article of mine, "Golden Liars of the Golden West," published by *Vanity Fair* in 1931. I hadn't met Nat Straw then, but I had heard his yarn about riding the bear. It was told to me by a hunter of mountain lions on the Double Circle Ranch who credited it to Nat Straw. This is the way Nat Straw had told it:

"The best bear I ever owned or saw was a grizzly cub I captured. It

---

[1]The manuscripts from which this story was taken are owned by the Harry Ransom Humanities Research Center, The University of Texas at Austin.

grew up so intelligent and gentle-natured and powerful that I broke him to ride. Before long I got him trained to help me hunt other bears. By the time he was three years old he was a regular monster in size.

"Generally I rode him with a hackamore (halter) and rope reins, but he was so quick at understanding which way I wanted him to go and so ready to respond that I really didn't need reins. I never used a saddle on him, just rode bareback. He had a soft-cushioned back that was as comfortable as a rocking chair. On account of him being so cunning and such a good trailer, I named him Geronimo.

"I didn't need no dogs after Geronimo and me got to working together. He'd wind a trail, and then about the time it got real hot I'd slip off and crawl along next to Geronimo's side so that the bear we were hunting could not see me. Of course, it would not run from another bear. Then when we got up close, I'd take aim under old Geronimo's belly and kill the bear.

"Well, one day I rode out without a gun. I never had any idea of using it. I was just riding Geronimo around kinder for exercise when we struck about as big a bear as ever you heard of. I shore didn't want to let it go, and right then Geronimo showed his sense. He seemed to know that I didn't have a gun and that I wanted that big bear.

"I slipped the hackamore off his head right quick and told him to make his own kill. He just waddled on up to the stranger as if he wanted to talk to him, me being off there behind some bushes. Then when everything was set right, he gave that other bear a slap and a hug, and I don't know what happened next.

"That strange bear was a fighter from Bitter Creek. The two clinched and battered and wallered, and the fur was flying so thick and the bushes was cracking so hard that I couldn't see or hear straight. I did see that they were the same size and color and everything.

"But directly it appeared to me that Geronimo was getting the worst of the tussle—and there I was without a thing to help him with. I'd heard about the man who knocked a half-ton grizzly down, then rammed his bowie knife into the critter's foaming mouth and cut his tongue out. But I didn't have a knife of any kind.

"I was thinking hard what to do. Then it came to me that Geronimo would obey me if I gave him an order. I decided right there to call him off, jump a-straddle of him, and burn the breezes for home. I wouldn't have had Geronimo hurt for all the bears in the Mogollon Mountains.

"Well, I yelled out 'Geronimo.' At this the bears kinda slacked their battle.

"I yelled, 'Geronimo' a second time, loud like that.

"He turned towards me, and then I saw on his face a frozen expression I'd never seen before. I didn't see it long though. I made a leap for his back like a buck deer a-hitting the brush in the hunting season, and roweling his side with my spur I yelled for him to git. There wasn't no time for putting the hackamore back on him. By golly, you out to have seen that bear leave Cheyenne.

"We went tearing through oak brush and under scrub juniper and over fallen pine logs as if they was nothing but weeds. It was all I could do to stay on that bear, and not hardly any of my skin was staying on me. I'd a jumped off but from the sounds going on I judged the other bear was tearing after us. I didn't have time to look back to see.

"I've heard about the clatter wheels of hell being noisy, but I tell you the landslide we made was noisier than any kind of clatter wheels ever invented. I just hadn't any idea that Geronimo could be so reckless. I tried talking to him to hold him up, but it seemed the more I talked the more reckless he got.

"Then I tried reaching over and catching him by the right ear. When I did, I saw that about half of it was gone, not from any recent fight either. The skin was haired over. Well sir, right then the facts dawned on me. Geronimo wasn't gotched in the ear at all. I had mounted the wrong bear and ridden him a mile down Cienega Canyon. I didn't wait until he stopped to get off. I just fell off.

"I'd had such a bait of bear-riding that I never did mount Geronimo again. He came into camp all right and lived with me for years after that. But somehow I had just lost all confidence in him as a saddle animal, and he was the last bear I ever tried to ride."

At the time that this yarn was published . . . a friend of mine named Clarence Insall was covering lots of country gathering walnut roots to ship to France so that they could be made into briar pipes and shipped back to the United States for us smokers. He knew Nat Straw and, expecting to see him on the Gila River, took him a copy of the magazine making vain use of his name. After reading the piece, Nat Straw told the walnut root hunter to tell me that he certainly was not the only liar in the West.

Six years or so later, I was in New Mexico trailing down the Lost Adams Diggings, one of the happiest trails I was ever on. After having received, high up in the Mogollons, among the mountain tops, authentic tidings of things both visible and invisible, I went to Santa Fe on the road to Texas. Here I ran into two old friends, Stokley Ligon, naturalist, and Dub Evans, rancher and lion-hunter.

When I told them what I'd been doing, they said, "The idea of being on the trail of the Lost Adams Diggings and not seeing Nat Straw! Why, Nat Straw took up with a Navajo squaw so he could learn the tribal secrets of the Adams gold. You've simply got to see him before you leave New Mexico. He's got more lore of the Adams Diggings than any other man in the country!"

I found Nat Straw on the Gila River above Silver City, living with a young couple. Out a short distance from their house, I camped under the biggest cottonwood tree I've ever seen.

Nat Straw. Address him: Some canyon in New Mexico between the eastern slopes of the Black Range and the western edge of the Mogollon Mountains. He'll be down on the Gila River in the winter, though. After being snowed up with his burros one time for endless months, not even a bird left in the high mountains, he's had no hankering to repeat the experience.

"From my earliest infancy," he told me, "I longed to be in wild places with wild men and wild animals." This longing, which never subsided, was first realized when, at the age of eight in Minnesota, he was captured by Sioux Indians during the Civil War. He lived long enough with them to learn their language and like, better than any other food he has ever tasted, their preparation of buffalo meat. An old squaw had his leg strapped to a log and was tatooing on it a tribal design, when soldiers stormed the camp and rescued him.

As a man, Nat Straw took up with the Navajos, and mastered their tongue, their lore, and at least one of their women. He has been a chuck-wagon cook as well as a cowboy. Once, he had a good little stake, but he lost it all in one night, when a blizzard killed thirty five hundred sheep for him. Prevailingly, however, he has been a hunter and trapper of predatory animals in the Gila Wilderness Area.

Off and on for half a century, he prospected a considerable part of the Rocky Mountains and he knows ten thousand places "where the Lost Adams Diggings ain't." He said he had lost all interest in the Adams Diggings and had written high up on an aspen: "The Adams Diggings is a shadowy naught that lies in the valley of fanciful thought."

Education has nothing to do with the rare faculty possessed by a few individuals of making whatever they talk about interesting. Nat Straw had that quality and he had cultivated it. If a person rode up to his lone—and always clean—camp, even on a summer night he would likely see a blazing fire, by the light of which Nat Straw was contriving to read a good book. He was a frontiersman of the old rock, but not all pioneers have been illiterate.

When I met him and listened to him talk for two nights and a day, under the gigantic cottonwood on the Gila, he was already eighty-two years old. In his old age he had lost the zest of his more vigorous years for entertaining yarns. What Nat Straw really wanted to tell me were factual experiences with bears that were stranger than any possible invention. He is a remarkably mild man, but he did not know how many bears he had killed. "I wish I had kept count," he said. He killed most of them for the cow and sheep outfits who paid him to protect their stock. Nat said, "A bear will travel thirty miles to find a good harvest of acorns; he will graze on clover like a cow, and he will get as fat as a hog on pinon nuts, wild cherries, manzanita berries and other fruitage, but once let him get the taste of cow or sheep meat and after that he is a confirmed killer."

All kinds, conditions, and sizes of bears Nat Straw had hunted down. But the bear of bears, both as a predator and as a match for the deadliest rifleman that ever stalked the mountains, is the grizzly. Since old man Ben Lilly's death, Nat Straw is about the last of the grizzly bear hunters of the West.

Here is what Nat Straw told me about some of his true experiences with bear in the Gila Wilderness Area:

Working for many years as destroyer of predatory animals for the V Cross T, Flying V, Heart Bars, XSX, and other outfits, and over the vast sheep ranges controlled by Eduardo Otero, I was more trapper than hunter. I was paid, by bounty, only for the wolves, bears, and panthers killed, and I learned that I could collect more through traps than otherwise. For a time I was a Government trapper also.

Now, a bear does not have very good eyes, compared with those of an Indian, an antelope, or a buzzard. He has wonderfully acute hearing. His nose is better than his ear, though it is not so sharp as that of the wolf, whether lobo or coyote. But all wild animals are guided by their sense of smell more than by any other sense. A lot that human beings don't know about themselves can be learned by studying the sense of smell in animals.

In the beginning I used deer meat for bait at bear traps. Many a time I have found where a bear had picked a trap up in one of his paws and turned it over, and then gone on into the place where the venison was placed and eaten it. I usually set two traps—one for the bear to turn over, or otherwise avoid, and one to surprise him.

I wouldn't think of baiting a trap with meat now—only scent. The mountain men were using scent bait when Kit Carson was a boy, but I never knew or heard of an Indian using it. A wild animal will flee the scent of a man quicker than the sight of him. Then, ADIOS! In an animal the final judgment and recognition of nearly anything is made through smell. Take a wolf that's been caught in a trap and has then escaped. That gives him a degree in higher education, so far as traps are concerned. He won't forget. His schoolteacher won't have to repeat the lesson to him.

In the same way that scents scare them and protect them, any animal can be lured and trapped and subdued by scent, as by nothing else.

I used to rub onion on my hands and shoes and the parts of my

clothes that bushes touch against, so as to kill the human odor. This
was many years ago. Then I read of a German who found out by
accident that while he had a little Toko musk on his body a bear
followed him ten miles through the Black Forest.

Toko musk is from China. I found that it cost thirty-one dollars an
ounce. I got a little of the tincture of it and mixed it with oil of
rhodium. Every trapper has his secret scent. I am telling mine. You
can rub that mixture of oil of rhodium and Toko musk on your hands
and on a rope, and then walk up to the wildest bronc, catch him, and
lead him around like a pet.

Well, about 1904, while I was trapping in the White Creek country
for Johnny Converse of the Heart Bars, I rubbed some of the mixture
on my shoes one day and made a round of not more than three miles.
There was no snow on the ground. I slept in a tepee tent with the flaps
open. That night the presence rather than the noise of something
awoke me. I always slept with my rifle by my side. I reached for it very,
very easily, at the same time looking out without moving my head. I
could see that the fire in front of the tent had burned to ashes. I could
also see a manlike bulk in the door. I took this bulk to be a bear
standing up. At some slight movement of mine in getting the gun up,
he turned and put his paws on a log close to the tent door. I let him
have a bullet that made him fall and go to groaning and, in his wrath,
gnawing the log. The next bullet finished him. He was a big brown
bear. After that I didn't put any more scent on my shoes to lure
animals into following me to camp.

Like the bad man, the grizzly was always looking for trouble. Both
found it. Both are virtually gone now. The grizzly was the only animal
of America that did look for trouble. He was the king and the bully of
the animal world. Whoever says he would not attack man unless
bothered, don't know. Grizzlies, like other wild animals, tend to fear
men; human beings tend to be decent, but nobody who knows either
kind of these two animals has to go far to find exceptions. I hesitate to
tell what I have experienced, for fear of not being believed, but a man
can't deny sixty years of his life.

My narrowest escape, I guess, was from an enormous grizzly I had trapped. You don't fasten those gigantic steel traps to a tree, but to a clog, or a piece of log that drags. If the trap is fixed, the animal is likely to gnaw or pull his foot off. With a drag, he will move slow leaving a distinct trail.

Well, I found my trap gone, and sign along the trail told me the grizzly was a giant. I followed, slow and cautious, for a trapped bear is always in a great rage and is apt to show up and charge a man at any minute. The trail went down into a narrow zigzag canyon and through solid sandstone, with many sharp corners. Turning any one of them, I might step into the jaws of the bear. Common sense told me I had better not follow, but I was like a hunting dog hot on the trail. I would not turn back. The sandstone walls had in them many crevices, some just about wide enough for a coon to squeeze into, some high enough to admit a man, and some wide and deep. I was walking soft and I was halting at every bend and taking a good look ahead before I went on.

After a very sharp corner, I halted and stuck my head around to look. I almost stuck it into the grizzly's face. Perhaps he had smelled me. Anyway, he seemed to be expecting somebody. Before I could move, he lunged at me on all fours, steel trap and pain forgotten. I can't swear that his mouth was open, but I think it was. His head and fore parts were covered with blood and red foam. He had broken out all his teeth biting the trap, and the steel had cut deep into his gums.

When he charged, I darted into the first of those cuts in the canyon wall at hand. I don't know if I'd seen it before. It was right at me. It was just wide enough to admit my body, and it was not more than three feet deep into the sandstone. By the time I was flattened against the back wall, the bear, standing now on his hind legs, was pawing into the opening. The trap was on his right foot, leaving his south paw free. His bloody jaws, under beady, blood-shot eyes, were so close to me that when he tossed and breathed, the red foam covered my own face. His great paw raked within four or five inches of my face and breast, but the opening was too small for his breast to squeeze through. I kept my long rifle held perpendicular against my body, and I sucked in my stomach until it was against my backbone.

There was no room for me to raise the muzzle of the rifle to shoot; if any part of the gun came within grasp of the bear's paw, he would, I knew, tear it from me and probably break it.

I have never heard a bear growl, although I have read many times about their growl. A bear will clamp his jaws. He will kind of whine and hum at the same time, and when you hear that sound you had better get your shooting irons. He will roar. It is impossible to describe the rage of a great grizzly tortured by pain and mad for vengeance. There he stands, weighing more than half a ton, as powerful for his size as an ant is for his, and his power doubled and trebled by a rage inconceivable to man.

This grizzly flung the big steel trap on his right forearm against the stone facing of the crevice into which I was backed. He seemed forgetful of the pain. With his free paw he tried to break off chunks of stone. He bit at the stone with the jaws he had already torn on steel. He tried to squeeze gradually into the opening. He lunged into it and it seemed to me that the claws of his hand, as big as a ham, reached an inch or two nearer my body. People who have not had opportunity to observe cannot realize what power is in the hand, or paw, of a great bear. I have seen a grizzly slap lightly the head of a bull, and knock him to the ground with a broken neck.

I do not know how long I stayed in that rock crevice, facing the grizzly. It seemed hours, but it might not have been more than fifteen minutes. He did not relent for a second, so as to give me time to raise the gun and shoot. It looked to me as if the rocks would melt under his white-hot rage. I thought of the way I'd heard of Apaches spread-eagling a man down on his back, face up, tying beside him a big rattlesnake by a rawhide thong just short of striking distance, and then, while they enraged the snake, dropping water, drop by drop, on the rawhide until it at last expanded enough for the fangs to enter the face of the man. I thought of this and other slow ways of death. When I was a boy I had read Poe's story of "The Pit and the Pendulum."

Finally the bear stood off a second, seemingly to consider some new way of attack. Until I went to raise the gun, I did not realize how weak I had become. As I raised it, the grizzly came again, but he was too late to miss a shot in his belly and not quick enough to grasp the barrel. A bear that's merely shot through the belly can live a long, long time. If possible, this one now became more furious than ever, but I soon saw that he was weakening. Before long he kind of hunkered down. I put a bullet through his head. When I shot that last time, his eyes were closed. Now they opened, like a bear's always open when he's dead. I had to sit down a long time before I had strength to stick him and start skinning. He was a monster.

PART IV

Recreations and Requiems

The Age of Appreciation, 1920–1986

Zane Grey, his son Romer, and two bears. Zane acrimoniously left Arizona when the new Arizona Game and Fish Commission refused him permission to hunt bears out of season. He later developed an anti-hunting attitude and confined his outdoor interests to fishing. Photograph courtesy of Norman Mead.

Colorado Trails

Zane Grey

ca. 1922

Zane Grey was the Louis L'Amour of his day, writing over thirty best-selling western novels, including such classics as *Code of the West, Under the Tonto Rim,* and *Riders of the Purple Sage.* Grey was an avid outdoorsman and hunted widely in his beloved Southwest. In this selection,[1] first published in his nonfiction work *Tales of Lonely Trails* (New York: Blue Ribbon Books, 1922), which was recently reissued by Northland Press (1986), Grey describes a bear hunt in the Flattop Mountains of Colorado. The Flattops are a large rolling subalpine mesa in north-central Colorado near the headwaters of the Colorado River. Grey shows sympathy for the black bear, which his hunting group eventually trees, and refuses to shoot him, but then joins in energetically as the hunters spot and give chase to a grizzly bear. His ambivalence toward bears and bear hunting is representative of the prevailing attitudes of his age: hunters enjoying the thrill of the chase but finding the actual kill distasteful. Later in life he disavowed all hunting and confined his outdoor passion to fishing, but not until he had hunted bears and lions for many years from a cabin he built in Arizona under the Tonto Rim. The change in Grey's attitude toward

---

[1]Permission for publication of this story was granted by Northland Press, Flagstaff, Arizona, and Zane Grey, Inc.

hunting is representative of the larger change that occurred in national perspective on the sport during his lifetime. 🦌

One afternoon a rancher visited our camp and informed us that he had surprised a big black bear eating the carcass of a dead cow.

"Good! We'll have a bear tomorrow night," declared Teague, in delight. "We'll get him even if the trail is a day old. But he'll come back tonight."

Early the next morning the young rancher and three other boys rode into camp, saying they would like to go with us to see the fun. We were glad to have them, and we rode off through the frosted sage that crackled like brittle glass under the hoofs of the horses. Our guide led toward a branch of a park, and when we got within perhaps a quarter of a mile Teague suggested that R. C. and I go ahead on the chance of surprising the bear. It was owing to this suggestion that my brother and I were well ahead of the others. But we did not see any bear near the carcass of the cow. Old Jim and Sampson were close behind us, and when Jim came within forty yards of that carcass he put his nose up with a deep and ringing bay, and he shot by us like a streak. He never went near the dead cow! Sampson bayed like thunder and raced after Jim.

"They're off!" I yelled to R. C. "It's a hot scent! Come on!"

We spurred our horses and they broke across the open park to the edge of the woods. Jim and Sampson were running straight with noses high. I heard a string of yelps and bellows from our rear.

"Look back!" shouted R. C.

Teague and the cowboys were unleashing the rest of the pack. It surely was great to see them stretch out, yelping wildly. Like the wind they passed us. Jim and Sampson headed into the woods with deep bays. I was riding Teague's best horse for this sort of work and he understood the game and plainly enjoyed it. R. C.'s horse ran as fast in the woods as he did in the open. This frightened me, and I yelled to R. C. to be careful. I yelled to deaf ears. That is the first great risk—a rider is not going to be careful! We were right on top of Jim and Sampson with the pack clamoring mad music just behind. The forest rang. Both horses hurdled logs, sometimes two at once. My old lion chases with Buffalo Jones had made me skillful in dodging branches and snags, and sliding knees back to avoid knocking them against trees. For a mile the forest was comparatively open, and here we had a grand and ringing run. I received two hard knocks, was unseated once, but held on, and I got a stinging crack in the face from a branch. R. C. added several more black-and-blue spots to his already spotted anatomy, and he missed, just by an inch, a solid snag that would have broken him in two. The pack stretched out in wild staccato chorus, the little Airedales literally screeching. Jim got out of our sight and then Sampson. Still it was even more thrilling to follow by sound rather than sight. They led up a thick, steep slope. Here we got into trouble in the windfalls of timber and the pack drew away from us, up over the mountain. We were half way up when we heard them jump the bear. The forest seemed full of strife and bays and yelps. We heard the dogs go down again to our right, and as we turned we saw Teague and the others strung out along the edge of the park. They got far ahead of us. When we reached the bottom of the slope they were out of sight, but we could hear them yell. The hounds were working around on another slope, from which craggy rocks loomed above the timber. R. C.'s horse lunged across the park and appeared to be running off from mine. I was a little to the right, and when my horse got under way, full speed, we had the bad luck to plunge suddenly into soft ground. He went to his knees, and I sailed out of the saddle full twenty feet, to alight all spread out and to slide like a plow. I did not seem to be hurt. When I got up my horse was coming and he appeared to be patient with me, but he was in a hurry. Before we got across the wet place R. C. was out of sight. I decided that instead of worrying about him I had better think about myself. Once on hard ground my horse fairly charged into the woods and we broke brush and branches as if they had been punk. It was again open forest, then a rocky slope, and then a flat ridge with aisles between the trees. Here I heard the melodious notes of Teague's hunting horn, and following that, the full chorus of the hounds. They had treed the bear. Coming into still more open forest, with rocks here and there, I caught sight of

R. C. far ahead, and soon I had glimpses of the other horses, and lastly, while riding full tilt, I spied a big, black, glistening bear high up in a pine a hundred yards or more distant.

Slowing down I rode up to the circle of frenzied dogs and excited men. The boys were all jabbering at once. Teague was beaming. R. C. sat on his horse, and it struck me that he looked sorry for the bear.

"Fifteen minutes!" ejaculated Teague, with a proud glance at Old Jim standing with forepaws up on the pine.

Indeed it had been a short and ringing chase.

All the time while I fooled around trying to photograph the treed bear, R. C. sat there on his horse, looking upward.

"Well, gentlemen, better kill him," said Teague, cheerfully. "If he gets rested he'll come down."

It was then I suggested to R. C. that he do the shooting.

"Not much!" he exclaimed.

The bear looked really pretty perched up there. He was as round as a barrel and black as jet and his fur shone in the gleams of sunlight. His tongue hung out, and his plump sides heaved, showing what a quick, hard run he had made before being driven to the tree. What struck me most forcibly about him was the expression in his eyes as he looked down at those devils of hounds. He was scared. He realized his peril. It was utterly impossible for me to see Teague's point of view.

"Go ahead—and plug him," I replied to my brother. "Get it over."

"You do it," he said.

"No, I won't."

"Why not— I'd like to know?"

"Maybe we won't have so good a chance again—and I want you to get your bear," I replied.

"Why it's like—murder," he protested.

"Oh, not so bad as that," I returned, weakly. "We need the meat. We've not had any game meat, you know, except ducks and grouse."

"You won't do it?" he added, grimly.

"No, I refuse."

Meanwhile the young ranchers gazed at us with wide eyes and the expression on Teague's honest, ruddy face would have been funny under other circumstances.

"That bear will come down an' mebbe kill one of my dogs," he protested.

"Well, he can come for all I care," I replied, positively, and I turned away.

I heard R. C. curse low under his breath. Then followed the spang of his .35 Remington. I wheeled in time to see the bear straining upward in terrible convulsions, his head pointed high, with blood spurting from his nose. Slowly he swayed and fell with a heavy crash.

The next bear chase we had was entirely different medicine.

Off in the basin under the White Slides, back of our camp, the hounds struck a fresh track and in an instant were out of sight. With the cowboy Vern setting the pace we plunged after them. It was rough country. Bogs, brooks, swales, rocky little parks, stretches of timber full of windfalls, groves of aspens so thick we could scarcely squeeze through—all these obstacles soon allowed the hounds to get away. We came out into a large park, right under the mountain slope, and here we sat our horses listening to the chase. That trail led around the basin and back near to us, up the thick green slope, where high up near a ledge we heard the pack jump this bear. It sounded to us as if he had been roused out of a sleep.

"I'll bet it's one of the big grizzlies we've heard about," said Teague.

That was something to my taste. I have seen a few grizzlies. Riding to higher ground I kept close watch on the few open patches up on the slope. The chase led toward us for a while. Suddenly I saw a big bear with a frosted coat go lumbering across one of these openings.

"Silvertip! Silvertip!" I yelled at the top of my lungs. "I saw him!"

My call thrilled everybody. Vern spurred his horse and took to the right. Teague advised that we climb the slope. So we made for the timber. Once there we had to get off and climb on foot. It was steep, rough, very hard work. I had on chaps and spurs. Soon I was hot, laboring, and my heart began to hurt. We all had to rest. The baying of the hounds inspirited us now and then, but presently we lost it.

Teague said they had gone over the ridge and as soon as we got up to the top we would hear them again. We struck an elk trail with fresh elk tracks in it. Teague said they were just ahead of us. I never climbed so hard and fast in my life. We were all tuckered out when we reached the top of the ridge. Then to our great disappointment we did not hear the hounds. Mounting we rode along the crest of this wooded ridge toward the western end, which was considerably higher. Once on a bare patch of ground we saw where the grizzly had passed. The big, round tracks, toeing in a little, made a chill go over me. No doubt of its being a silvertip!

We climbed and rode to the high point, and coming out upon the summit of the mountain we all heard the deep, hoarse baying of the pack. They were in the canyon down a bare grassy slope and over a wooded bench at our feet. Teague yelled as he spurred down. R. C. rode hard in his tracks.

But my horse was new to this bear chasing. He was mettlesome, and he did not want to do what I wanted. When I jabbed the spurs into his flanks he nearly bucked me off. I was looking for a soft place to light when he quit. Long before I got down that open slope Teague and R. C. had disappeared. I had to follow their tracks. This I did at a gallop, but now and then lost the tracks, and had to haul in to find them. If I could have heard the hounds from there I would have gone on anyway. But once down in the jack-pines I could hear neither yell or bay. The pines were small, close together, and tough. I hurt my hands, scratched my face, barked my knees. The horse had a habit of suddenly deciding to go the way he liked instead of the way I guided him, and when he plunged between saplings too close together to permit us both to go through, it was exceedingly hard on me. I was worked into a frenzy. Suppose R. C. should come face to face with that old grizzly and fail to kill him! That was the reason for my desperate hurry. I got a crack on the head that nearly blinded me. My horse grew hot and began to run in every little open space. He could scarcely be held in. And I, with the blood hot in me too, did not hold him hard enough.

It seemed miles across that wooded bench. But at last I reached another slope. Coming out upon a canyon rim I heard R. C. and

Teague yelling, and I heard the hounds fighting the grizzly. He was growling and threshing about far below. I had missed the tracks made by Teague and my brother, and it was necessary to find them. That slope looked impassable. I rode back along the rim, then forward. Finally I found where the ground was plowed deep and here I headed my horse. He had been used to smooth roads and he could not take these jumps. I went forward on his neck. But I hung on and spurred him hard. The mad spirit of that chase had gotten into him too. All the time I could hear the fierce baying and yelping of the hounds, and occasionally I heard a savage bawl from the bear. I literally plunged, slid, broke a way down that mountain slope, riding all the time, before I discovered the footprints of Teague and R. C. They had walked, leading their horses. By this time I was so mad I would not get off. I rode all the way down that steep slope of dense saplings, loose rock slides and earth, and jumble of splintered cliff. That he did not break my neck and his own spoke the truth about that roan horse. Despite his inexperience he was great. We fell over one bank, but a thicket of aspens saved us from rolling. The avalanches slid from under us until I imagined that the grizzly would be scared. Once as I stopped to listen I heard bear and pack farther down the canyon— heard them above the roar of a rushing stream. They went on and I lost the sounds of fight. But R. C.'s clear thrilling call floated up to me. Probably he was worried about me.

Then before I realized it I was at the foot of the slope, in a narrow canyon bed, full of rocks and trees, with the din of roaring water in my ears. I could hear nothing else. Tracks were everywhere, and when I came to the first open place I was thrilled. The grizzly had plunged off a sandy bar into the water, and there he had fought the hounds. Signs of that battle were easy to read. I saw where his huge tracks, still wet, led up the opposite sandy bank.

Then, down stream, I did my most reckless riding. On level ground the horse was splendid. Once he leaped clear across the brook. Every plunge, every turn I expected to bring me upon my brother and Teague and that fighting pack. More than once I thought I heard the spang of the .35 and this made me urge the roan faster and faster.

The canyon narrowed, the stream-bed deepened. I had to slow down to get through the trees and rocks. And suddenly I was overjoyed to ride pell-mell upon R. C. and Teague with half the panting hounds. The canyon had grown too rough for the horses to go farther and it would have been useless for us to try on foot. As I dismounted, so sore and bruised I could hardly stand, old Jim came limping in to fall into the brook where he lapped and lapped thirstily. Teague threw up his hands. Old Jim's return meant an ended chase. The grizzly had eluded the hounds in that jumble of rocks below.

"Say, did you meet the bear?" queried Teague, eyeing me in astonishment and mirth.

Bloody, dirty, ragged and wringing wet with sweat I must have been a sight. R. C., however, did not look so very immaculate, and when I saw he also was lame and scratched and black I felt better.

The Last Grizzly

Elliot Barker

1923

No anthology of Southwest bear stories would be complete without a contribution by Elliot Barker. Rancher, professional trapper of predators, Forest Ranger, Forest Supervisor, Director of the New Mexico Game and Fish Department for more than twenty years, wilderness advocate and author, Elliot Barker is one of the very few who knew and killed Southwest grizzlies but lived to regret his actions. Having passed away in 1987 at the age of 101, Barker will be long remembered as one of New Mexico's foremost conservationist figures.

The following story is one of several first-hand accounts of grizzlies in his charming book, *Beatty's Cabin,* published in 1953 by the University of New Mexico Press. In a 1963 letter to Levon Lee, Director of the New Mexico Game and Fish Department, published in Bessie Doak and Edgar Haynes's *The Grizzly Bear: Portraits from Life* (University of Oklahoma Press, 1966), Barker stated his belief that the grizzly was a natural predator on elk and that when the elk was extirpated from New Mexico the grizzly turned to killing livestock. Although he personally regretted that the grizzly *had* to be exterminated, he felt that there was no possibility of coexistence between livestock and the Great Bear.

The ambiguity of attitude between the practical nature of a cattleman and the aesthetic pleasures of a conservationist is succinctly expressed in this short account of the last grizzly in the Sangre de Cristos, once prime grizzly country and one of his final Southwest holdouts. The hide of the bear is now on display in the main office of the New Mexico Game and Fish Department in Santa Fe. ✹

Skipper Viles summer grazed his cattle in the Round Mountain and Beatty's Park area and built a two-room cabin a mile below Beatty's [cabin] for the cowboys' summer headquarters. The cabin, recently torn down and replaced by a better one, has always been known as Viles' Cabin.

In 1923, I was operating a mountain ranch on Sapello Creek and summer grazing my cattle in the Beaver Creek and Big Burn country. A big grizzly bear came into Skipper's range and killed some cattle. Skipper tried to trap him but the old bear was a smart one and had learned what traps were and refused to be caught. When he couldn't find a way to get to the carcass without getting caught, he would go kill another cow. I heard of all this and, although it was fifteen miles over there, I was on the lookout for him to come to my range and sample some of my beef.

Sure enough, one day I rode over to Beaver Creek and found he had been there and killed a two-year-old steer near the head of the north fork of Beaver, and a young cow three miles below, right near our branding corral. He had eaten a big meal out of the belly and rump of the first one, but the second he had just killed for fun. I thought he might come back so rode to the ranch and got some bear traps and a camp outfit so I could camp near the cattle. The Koogler boys, neighboring ranchers, came over and we set the traps. The old fellow didn't come back that night so the others went home. I took my three Airedales and tried to follow him, or at least find out which way he had gone and where he might strike next.

We found his big, foot-long track headed right down the dusty trail along Beaver Creek and followed it four miles to the junction with Hollinger Canyon. There he had turned right back up the Hollinger, sticking to the trail most of the way, his claw marks showing three inches ahead of the toe pads at every step. At the falls, five miles up the canyon, he turned out to the right and went up through the Big Burn to the top of the range. By then it was getting late and the track was still two days old, so I turned back and rode the eight long mountain miles back to the ranch.

That night I phoned Skipper Viles to be on the lookout for the grizzled old stock killer for he was headed back his way. Skipper reported that the bear had come back to one of his previous kills the night before and gotten caught in a trap waiting for his big foot, and that he had shot him that morning. That, as far as I know, was the last grizzly bear of the Pecos high country. From time to time, there have been reports of tracks of a grizzly being seen but certainly none lives there, and it could be only one occasionally passing through.

At the time I was a bit jealous of Skipper because he, not I, had killed the bear. Now, since it proved to be the last one, I am mighty glad I didn't kill it. Mrs. Viles still has the rug and it is really a nice one.

There Goes a Bear— and—It's a Grizzly

Carlos Mateo Bailón G.

Chihuahua Hunting and Shooting Club,
May 20, 1955

The following account of a bear hunt in Chihuahua by Carlos Bailón was contributed by Ing. José Treviño, a Mexican biologist who received a Master's Degree from New Mexico State University for his work on pronghorn antelope. Bailón, a Mexican sportsman, describes a bear hunt in the Sierra del Nido while grizzlies were still present in those mountains. The original version was translated from the Spanish by James K. Evans.

Bailón's discussion indirectly hints at some previously unsuspected causes for the grizzly's demise in the Sierra del Nido. The vast holdings of the Terrenates family, a long-time target of land reform programs, were taken over by small ranching operations in the 1950s. The hinterlands, no longer guarded by the haciendas of feudal landlords, became increasingly available to the public. The effect of large numbers of hunters, insufficiently regulated and policed by game laws, is obvious in the narration. Although a grizzly is not bagged on this trip, Bailón's descriptions of the hunt (and of another expedition on which a grizzly *is* killed) provide insights into the dangers of permitting large numbers of amateur bear hunters into the habitat of a relict grizzly population. There have been no confirmed reports of grizzlies in the Sierra del Nido since 1960. 🌿

Terrenates, the rich hacienda, was the home of abundant wildlife, a paradise for the lucky hunters who had the good fortune to hunt its lands. Throughout its mountains, irregular and deep, three varieties of bear abounded: the grizzly, the black, and the cinnamon.[1] There also existed fabulous flocks of wild turkeys, plenty of white-tailed deer, and, in its extensive plains, immense herds of antelope as well as mule deer; packs of ferocious wolves and mountain lions that decimated the livestock herds; as well as several other minor kinds of wildlife—all using the range to the envy of every hunter, since permission to enter these lands to hunt was granted only rarely. Sometimes it was because the owners were "Gringos," and sometimes it was because they were Mexicans who, being influential and very aloof, did not allow even the wealthy to hunt except those with influence and those recommended for their fondness for sport hunting ($). For my part, I belonged and still belong to the first group, the "peluza," those who pay as they go; therefore, I had never gone hunting on those lands.

Thus, the years passed—including several years of intense drought which decimated a large part of the fauna. The use of locoweed contributed to the decline in numbers of many valuable species.

Currently, one can still bag one or another record-book specimen, but to get an exceptional animal is like finding a needle in a haystack. Year after year during the hunting seasons, however, hunters tramp through the mountains, praying to all the saints to help them find that "needle."

Two years ago I was one of those hunters—furtively. I went into the deep, rough canyons that form part of the mountain range with no one for company but my likable and experienced guide, a Tarahumara Indian who, more acculturated than most, was quite enthusiastic about bear hunting. This magnificent guide is very well known to the hunters of northern Mexico; we call him "Crucito" (surname Gutiérrez). He is, indeed, an excellent and magnificent guide.

[1] A common misapprehension of Mexican and earlier American bear hunters. There were, in fact, only two species of bear in the Southwest—the grizzly and the black bear, with the black bear commonly in brown pelage and colloquially called the "Cinnamon Bear."—Eds.

Not one of my hunting buddies was able to go with me on this sport-hunting adventure. It was, therefore, no trouble for me just to take off and go hunting alone, to San Lorenzo and from there to the mountains of Terrenates. I would thus be calming the little worm of my ambition by getting to know these "game preserve" mountains for the benefit of those of us who make up the "peluza."

At San Lorenzo it was recommended that I go to the home of Sr. Apolonio Cuevas, who received me with all the hospitality and esteem for which the country people of northern Mexico are famous. This recommendation had been made by my especially good friend, Sr. José Luis Ibarvo, who knew my weakness for hunting; and so it was that I arrived at the home of Sr. Cuevas as though it was my own and as though we were old friends. Once I explained my intentions, he indicated that we should wait until morning to leave because I had arrived rather late and the horses we needed were running loose in the pasture.

I spent the rest of the afternoon getting acquainted with this lovable and picturesque community and taking advantage of the opportunity to make new friends. . . . Thus, I was offered the company of three other gentlemen to accompany me for a couple of days on my journey into the mountains.

By about noon the day after my arrival in San Lorenzo, all was ready for our expedition into the mountains. I left the village accompanied by a fine group of men: Don Apolonio Cuevas and his son Carlos, son Isaac Marquez, el "Guero" (Blondie) Cepeda; and, by a true coincidence, that very night the little Indian, Crucito Gutiérrez, had returned to the village. He had returned the previous night from a hunt on which he had been a guide for real red-blooded hunters like Bermudez, Queveda, and Chavez of Juaréz, who, year after year, go bear hunting at the opening of the season.

Thus it was that, in such agreeable company, I left for the Pajarito [Little Bird] mountains. We had to pass through these mountains and the Juan Largo range to get to the lands of Terrenates, where I hoped to fulfill my hunting ambition of so many years. We traveled all day and arrived quite late at a place called "Phillip's Eye" at which we were to spend the night. In this beautiful place we came across some

Mexican hunters whose guide was the expert and dynamic hunter and taxidermist, Sr. Alejandro Lopéz Escalera, a great friend of mine and a colleague in taxidermy, who introduced me to his patrons. According to what they told me, they had had very bad luck on this venture, as they had seen only a very few bear tracks in all the days they had been hunting. On other occasions they had bagged beautiful specimens of bears but, on this trip, Lady Luck had turned her back on them and they hadn't seen even a deer. When an engineer found out that I was going on this hunt alone with only my guide, he said to me, "You really have to be a hell of a hunting enthusiast to come alone to these mountains to hunt."

Early the next day we started out after saying goodbye to our overnight companions, whom I wished the best of luck. About noon we arrived at the "gate" to Juan Largo, and there I waited for my companions, since they were coming along behind with the pack animals while I had gone ahead in hopes of encountering some game. My companions were quite late catching up, as one of the horses, the one that carried my gear, had taken a liking to some of the alternative routes through the mountains and had strewn my belongings among the oaks and bushes wherever he went. When my companions joined me, they told me the bad news: several boxes of cartridges had broken open and their contents spilled, and they had only been able to recover part of them. Some other things had also been lost or rendered useless but, so what! These are the things that happen, are least planned for, and serve to spice up each adventure!

At the "gate" we unpacked the animals to give them a deserved rest and went about filling our bellies to replace the strength we had lost on the trail. Once we and our horses were rested and revitalized, I told my companions, "While you repack the horses I will go on ahead. Show me the way to go and I'll wait for you farther on." Once they had shown me the route, I got on my horse and left, with the hope of running across some game. I rode for about an hour without seeing so much as a lizard. I found a high point on the hillside and sat down to wait for my companions. A long time went by with no sign of them. I looked for them through my binoculars and—nothing! I was not able to locate them by any route. A thorn of doubt began to prick at me with the thought that perhaps they had chosen a different route, believing that I would give them an advantage, and thus they had passed me without my knowledge. I went a little farther in futile hope; evening was coming on and, realizing that fact, I decided to go back and try to pick up the tracks of their horses. I succeeded in running across them but, after following them quite a ways I lost them completely, since the grass and the hardness of the ground kept the hooves of the horses from making distinct tracks. So, being reasonably certain that I wasn't going to find them this way, I decided to go back to where I had left them—at the "gate" to Juan Largo, being certain that they would go back there to look for me.

On the way back I fired three shots from my rifle, hoping that my companions would hear them and come at once to get me. I rode slowly, looking for the slightest sign of my companions, but— nothing! All was silence around me. In some rocks on the side of the canyon I was riding through, I could see the head of a cute little fox which, with its ears pricked up, was watching my progress through its domain. I dismounted from my horse and went to try to take it. I carried my .22 pistol to shoot it with, since the rifle had only expanding bullets, and I didn't want to ruin the hide. I got close enough for a pistol shot, but, because I am such a klutz, I fumbled and didn't even scare the little beast. Nevertheless, he made a fast dive for his den and, just before he went in, he turned and it seemed that he stuck his tongue out at me and threw me a "comet" (flipped me a bird). A little farther on I came across a formidable rattlesnake which almost struck my horse's front foot, frightening the animal so that he nearly shied out from under me. I dismounted immediately and, with my .22 pistol, I riddled the horrible reptile, but not before teasing him with an oak stick, which he struck many times with real fury and with the rapidity of the shuttle of a sewing machine, and making him very angry. Once the brute was good and dead, I cut off the rattles (there were 12) and hung them on an oak limb.

About five minutes after I killed the snake, I heard a horse's hoofbeats behind me. I turned to see what I might be about to tangle with and was very glad to discover that it was one of my companions on his horse, coming at a full gallop toward where I was. It was Don Isaac.

"What happened, Mr. Bailón? Where did you go?"

"I was going to Juan Largo "gate," I told him. "I had already decided to spend the night there in the hopes that one of you would come there to look for me."

"Well, you know we thought you had gone the right way, so we didn't even look for your tracks until we arrived at the troughs and didn't see any sign of you; then we began to worry and said to ourselves, 'I'll bet our buddy got lost.' So we started out to look for you, with such good luck that, where you dismounted the first time, I found your tracks; I then followed them at full gallop until I saw where you got off to shoot the rattler; then I said to myself, 'He can't be much farther'—and so, in order to catch up with you, I hit a 'lope' again and found I wasn't wrong."

"I am very grateful to you for your interest and worry in looking for me, Don Isaac, as well as to the others," I answered in thanking him.

In a few moments we were reunited with our other companions who, by different routes, had been looking for me. After getting back together, we resumed our journey toward the place where we would spend the night, and where Carlos, Don Apolonio's son, had remained behind. When we arrived in camp, he had a hot pot of aromatic coffee ready for us. We passed a good part of that night talking about my "going astray," until it was time to rest and replenish our strength for the next day's journey.

We started out again the next morning, and by the time the first rays of the sun began to warm our backs, we had already covered quite a bit of ground. About 11 A.M. we had arrived at the place where we were to make our base camp. After the mules were unpacked, we prepared a little lunch so that we could go out in the evening and try to get a deer to supply our camp with fresh meat. When we started fixing our snack, I started making flour tortillas and Don Apolonio watched me awhile. Finally, he said to me, "Hey, Charlie! I thought you were like the majority of the 'tightwads' who come from the city to hunt and who, once here in the mountains, want everything done for them and even to be put to bed—but I see that you are different, since you know how to do things and don't like everything done for you."

"Thanks, Don Apolonio," I said, "but the fact is that 'hunger makes the pot stir' and, above all, no one should be dependent when he can help, and, mostly, you guys don't have any obligation to do these things, for the simple reason that you didn't come as my servants but as companions!"

El "Guero" Cepeda made some fried potatoes with green chili and when we were eating it, Crucito, the Tarahumarito, exclaimed, "Hot damn! This guiso's got cheese in it! Tastes great!"

We all laughed because, although the guiso was quite good, it didn't have any cheese in it at all.

That afternoon we split up in twos and went different ways. Crucito, being my paid guide, stayed with me and would remain with me after the others had all returned to San Lorenzo the following day.

We all returned to camp about dark without any luck at hunting. Everyone thought it was quite unusual that no one had seen so much as a single deer, since all my companions were accustomed to seeing many whitetail in these parts. They couldn't offer any explanation for the scarcity of game. For several hours we hung around the campfire shooting the breeze and trying to be witty and jolly, but not many jokes were told, since the lack of confidence in relation to me prevented them and me from giving full release to such jovial moments of amusement. However, we passed an amiable evening together which wound down at about 11 P.M., and moments later we were in the arms of Morpheus.

Crucito and I followed the tracks all morning without catching up with our quarry in those rugged mountains. It must have been about noon when I suggested that we rest awhile and have some lunch so we could pursue our purpose more enthusiastically in the afternoon.

After lunch (which was quite light) I handed my binoculars to Crucito and instructed him to scan the surrounding country thoroughly, since my eyes were not capable of prolonged use of the binoculars while those of Crucito could hold up well under this visual effort.

I want to clarify that Crucito is a guide who counts on his own hunting equipment: rifle, cartridges, binoculars (of a low power), traps of all sizes, and a tremendous amount of experience in the hunting of bears, mountain lion, wolf, and every kind of predatory mammal. He is also an expert at night hunting and knows how to distinguish very well the characteristics, shine, and other details of the eyes of each species of animal that the beam from the lantern reveals in the darkness. So, despite the fact that he is a humble "Tarahumarito," he is a great guide and companion in whom one can place complete confidence.

While I smoked a cigarette, Crucito scrutinized all the terrain in front of us and all around us without once lowering the binoculars. I was watching him and admiring his powerful eyes that endured such prolonged effort when suddenly he lowered the binoculars and pointing with his finger, calmly told me, "There goes a bear—and—it's a grizzly!"

"Where, Crucito?" I asked him.

"Look over that way, to your right," and he handed me the binoculars.

I searched hard in the direction he indicated, which was thick manzanita, but I couldn't see anything.

"Did you see him?" he asked.

"No, Crucito, I don't see him anywhere," I declared.

"Look a little to the right of that dry pine in the middle of that manzanita thicket. He's eating manzanita berries," and he pointed right at the spot.

Finally I saw it! It looked like a little monkey in the brush, since one moment I could see it and the next I couldn't, as it moved slowly from bush to bush. I watched it for quite awhile through the binoculars, and then I asked Crucito, "How far do you think it is from here to where the bear is?"

"Well, I expect about a kilometer," he answered.

"And which way would you like to go to get closer without his seeing or sensing us?"

"Look, I believe it'd be best if we go along the high line, but we'll have to make a wide circle," he declared.

"Okay, Crucito. Let's go the way you think best for getting me in place for a good shot as soon as possible."

It was exactly one o'clock in the afternoon when we started the stalk that would find us the best way to get as close as possible to the formidable beast, which, aware of our presence, kept an eye on us while it continued feeding calmly on the tasty manzanita fruits.

While we were making our stalk over the wide circle that we were obliged to follow, we jumped two huge buck deer, to which we paid no attention but kept on going to the place where we had a good, open view of the entire hillside where our coveted prey was.

It was still too far for a decent shot; therefore, we started scooting carefully down the difficult piney hillside, having to take thousands of precautions not to slip and fall on the abundant loose rocks. We went down the hill a ways and I decided to have another look at the formidable "barfoot." I realized that it wasn't a grizzly after all, but a precious specimen of "Cinnamon Bear," which was still carrying a few tufts of old, unshed hair, making him look like a grizzly at a distance. We watched him through the binoculars, almost face to face, since we could appreciate, in this fashion, his enormous body as he went about feeding on the manzanita berries—his enormous, hairy arms, whose strength destroys the thick limbs of pine, oak, madrone, and other plants while in quest of his dinner—and his enormous head with great patches of long hair around the jaws. There was no doubt that he was a beautiful specimen in all his savage splendor.

So we continued on down the steep slope until we couldn't get any closer without his seeing us and fleeing. We came to some big rocks and hid there expectantly, hoping to get another good view of the bear, since we had lost sight of him moments earlier, maybe because he had walked behind a thick mat of manzanita brush. I looked at my watch and found that it was five minutes before 2 P.M., that it had taken us 55 minutes to make the stalk thus far.

Completely rested and with my pulse down to normal, I waited, ready, with my scoped 30–06, for the big hairy bugger to show himself again. I stayed that way for another 15 minutes, which seemed to me like 15 centuries, in excited hopefulness. All the advantages were in my favor. The bear had not sensed our presence; the wind was in our favor; and the distance that we had calculated last had been at about 275 meters from canyonside to canyonside, a good distance for a well-aimed shot. I was resting my rifle across a boulder for best advantage (and for best control of my nerves).

I told Crucito to take several photos of the bear the next time it was visible, regardless of the distance. I continued scrutinizing the thicket until, all of a sudden, I saw him come out of a small ravine straight across the canyon from me. I got him in my scope and placed the cross hairs on the little hollow where the arms meet the chest. As soon as he stopped for an instant, I squeezed the trigger steadily and, in my imagination, I could already see him rolling into the bottom of the draw.

At the thunder of the shot I could see that he made a great leap over backwards and disappeared from my sight. I quickly jacked another round into the chamber and waited to see if he would reappear. About five seconds later I saw him going out the other side of the draw—then he stopped in a wide open clearing and turned broadside, giving me a perfect shot. I aimed at the elbow and fired again, but—he didn't fall! Then I realized that my shot had been a little too low. I quickly threw another round in, but now the bear was going up the other side of the canyon like the devil was after him. I kept shooting at the fleeing barfoot without touching him; I had been unlucky since, within a few instants, he was getting farther and farther out of reach of my rifle. Finally, he crossed the top of the ridge and was lost to me, along with all my hopes which, moments earlier, had made him mine.

"Such a disappointment! How angry it makes me, to let such a beautiful animal get away!" I said to Crucito. "Look, Crucito! Look how normal my pulse is! I didn't even get excited! That makes me all the more angry that I failed to get him!"

"Don't worry! Don't worry! We'll find another one and then you'll sure as hell knock him down," he answered me calmly.

"Hey, Crucito, did you take those pictures I told you to?"

"Aw, hell! I couldn't make the damn camera work, so I didn't get pictures," he answered ruefully.

"Well, all the better, I guess. This way I won't have the terrible memory of this failure upon looking at the pictures later on. It would just make me mad all over again for letting the bear get away."

Afterward we went to look at the place where the bear was when I first shot at him. When we got there, we realized that I had hit him, but the wound was rather superficial, as there was very little blood spilled. We followed the trail until we lost it. Then Crucito said, "He's gonna be hard to find, because of the way he's traveling. It'd take us four days to catch up with him. Believe me, one of Don Otavo's hunters shot a grizzly bear—it ran like hell and bled a lot and we chased him and looked for him all over these mountains for four days and never found him. But don't worry. Tomorrow we'll find another."

I wasn't consoled by this, but what choice did I have? Lady Luck had turned her back on me, and I had miscalculated the distance for the first two shots, causing me to shoot too low by scant millimeters. But that's hunting; when you are sure you have your quarry in the bag, it slips through your fingers.

We hunted bears for several more days, but fickle Old Lady Luck gave me only that one chance, and, when I failed, she didn't want to give me another.

Grizzlies of
the Sierra del Nido

A. Starker Leopold

1967

A. Starker Leopold, son of the venerated conservationist Aldo Leopold, was a respected wildlife biologist, heading the Zoology Department for many years at the Berkeley campus of California and authoring the classic study *Wildlife of Mexico* (1959). In this article, originally published in *Pacific Discovery,* the journal of the California Academy of Sciences, Leopold examines the status of the grizzly bear in the Sierra del Nido, an isolated mountain range in central Chihuahua.[1] Leopold first became aware of this relict grizzly population in conversation with Tucson big-game hunter Ernest E. Lee, who had successfully hunted the big bears in the Sierra del Nido in the 1930s. In 1957 Leopold and a field party from Berkeley's Museum of Vertebrate Zoology found a small but still viable population in the del Nido. Owing to the use of the potent predacide, Compound 1080, however, the population rapidly diminished. Compound 1080, an odorless, tasteless white salt, kills predators feeding on poisoned meat, and no grizzlies are known to have been taken in the area since 1960. The grizzly in the Sierra del Nido presents an interesting case study of how a country, despite having an official policy of preserving the

[1] For additional information the reader is referred to A. Starker Leopold, "Situación del oso plateado en Chihuahua," *Rev. Soc. Mexicana Hist. Nat.* 19: 115–20 (1958); and A. Starker Leopold, *Wildlife of Mexico* (Berkeley: University of California Press, 1959).

grizzly, condoned policies that ineluctably led to the animals' elimination. Such studies have implications for isolated grizzly bear populations in America, and for isolated predator populations elsewhere, whether the Abruzzo brown bear in Italy or the lion in Africa and India.[2] 🐾

In central Chihuahua, close beside the Pan-American Highway, a massive butte rises several thousand feet above the desert. From a passing automobile one can see the dark pines silhouetted along the rim. A jagged little mountain range extends off to the northwest for some 20 miles, where it drops abruptly to the desert. The Sierra del Nido, by virtue of its rough topography, has remained essentially a wilderness, though surrounded by cattle ranches and in places, by farming lands. The best evidence of the wilderness character of this little mountain oasis is that it supports the last known population of the southwestern grizzly bear.

At the time of initial exploration, the grizzly was common throughout the rough breaks and chaparral lands of northwestern Mexico and adjoining southwestern United States. James O. Pattie, the wandering beaver trapper, made his way through New Mexico, Arizona, and northwestern Mexico in the 1820s and had frequent encounters with the big bears. George F. Ruxton, an intrepid Englishman who rode northward through Mexico in 1846, spoke of grizzlies as being particularly common in the rough mountains of Chihuahua. He camped near the base of the Sierra del Nido on November 12, 1846, and commented on the presence of wolves. Because of encampments of hostile Apaches he did not linger there, nor had he any reason to enter the mountains. Many grizzly bears were encountered by members of the United States and Mexican Boundary Survey party that located the present international boundary in 1855. Dr. Kennerly, one of the naturalists of the survey party, described various adventures with the grizzlies. As late as 1892 the second International Boundary Survey found plenty of grizzlies along the

[2]The story that follows is reprinted from *Pacific Discovery,* the quarterly science magazine of the California Academy of Sciences.

Chihuahua–New Mexico border, and in 1899 Dr. E. W. Nelson collected several specimens near Colonia García in northwestern Chihuahua. But by then the bears were becoming scarce along the border. In 1932 the last known grizzly was killed in the Sierra Madre, despite the fact that much of the big cordillera was still essentially unaltered wilderness at that time. Long before that, the species was extinct in New Mexico and Arizona.[3]

This sequence of persecution and depletion of the bear populations throughout all of western North America south of Yellowstone makes more dramatic the survival of a small remnant of grizzlies in the Sierra del Nido, situated as it is immediately beside the main route of travel through Chihuahua, from the days of the Spanish Conquistadores to the era of the speeding Greyhound bus. As already implied, the explanation for the persistence of the bears lies in the topographic features of the area.

Central Chihuahua is essentially a cattle country. The great haciendas of the last century were broken up into smaller units after the Mexican Revolution of 1912, but change of ownership did not alter the basic nature of the country. The rough breaks of the Sierra del Nido and adjoining buttes like Cerro Campana have limited value in a range cattle operation because there is no stock drinking water except the tiniest of seep springs, and the country is too rough for the cowboys to muster cattle on horseback. A Mexican cowpuncher, who despises walking from the corral to the ranch house, is not likely to be found chasing cows around a mountain afoot. It has been the custom therefore, on ranches situated around these highlands, to maintain drift fences that preclude the ascent of range stock into the cumbres and breaks. There is very little timber in these highlands, nor have any important mineral discoveries been made. Mexican ranch folk do not idly go into rough mountains unless there is a financial motive. Lacking one, the little Sierra del Nido is rarely visited and the big bears have escaped attention. There they have persisted long after the more spacious but rolling timberlands to the west were overrun with

[3]The last known grizzlies in Arizona were killed in 1935 and 1939, and the last grizzly in New Mexico was killed in 1931 or 1935.—Eds.

loggers, miners, and grazing operations, and pretty well stripped of wildlife.

The continued existence of grizzlies in the Sierra del Nido was known locally, but escaped attention elsewhere until field parties of the Museum of Vertebrate Zoology, University of California, began investigating the status of wild animals in this part of Mexico. Mr. Ernest E. Lee of Tucson, Arizona reported to us that he and his brothers had killed several grizzlies in the Sierra del Nido in the 1930s, and one in 1941. Inquiry in Chihuahua City revealed two local hunters that had taken big bears there in the 1950s. Sr. Isaías T. Gracía killed a monstrous male on October 24, 1955, while deer hunting, and repeated on October 4, 1957, with an adult female. A local taxidermist, Alexandro Lopéz Escalera, possessed a grizzly cub captured in 1954, and he had photographs of several adult bears that he had killed previously.

The Museum of Vertebrate Zoology sent four field parties into the Sierra del Nido between 1957 and 1961. Subsequently, Dr. Adrey Borrell made several winter visits to the mountain, collecting additional vertebrates missed by the earlier field parties. No living grizzlies were seen by us, although we were very close on two occasions. But on the basis of tracks, other signs, and information derived from local ranchers, the following can be said about the status of the bear population. In 1957 the tracks of ten bears were found along the crest of the Sierra del Nido during a 10-day stay in June. Most of these were grizzlies, judging from track size. Some may have been made by black bears which do occur in this area in lesser numbers than grizzlies, according to local people. From this scant bit of evidence we guessed that the whole population in the Sierra del Nido, and adjoining Sierra Santa Clara and Cerro Campana, might run as high as 30 individual animals, though this figure may have been far from accurate either way. At that time inquiry among ranchers indicated that the grizzlies stayed in the mountains most of the time, descending to the lower slopes only in autumn during the acorn season. No one could recall any predation on livestock by the bears.

However, this serene state of affairs changed abruptly in 1961 when the rancher who owns the central sector of Sierra del Nido lost 16 head of cattle to bear predation. He surmised, probably correctly, that a single cranky old bear was responsible for this damage. But his response was to declare general war on all bears with an avowed purpose of extermination. Using traps, guns, and, worst of all, 1080 poison stations, the rancher has persecuted the animals, though precisely how many have been killed is not known. Poison stations were put out in the winters of 1961–62, 62–63, and 63–64, using 1080-treated meat baits obtained from the Oficina Sanitaria Panamericana.[4] Although in 1959 the grizzly bear was officially placed on the list of protected mammals in Mexico, and an even more formal proclamation of this event was issued by the President in July, 1960, the facts as noted in the field do not conform with the law. Observations in recent years by Adrey Borrell and by Alexandro Lopéz Escalera have uncovered very few tracks or other sign of bears. The population apparently is so low as to be nearing the extermination point.

What is the future of the Mexican grizzly? Can it be restored to a safe level to assure preservation of the breeding stock? In 1963 a proposal to the World Wildlife Fund was submitted by Rodolfo Hernandez Corzo, Chief of the Game Division of Mexico, asking for financial support to study the grizzly situation in the Sierra del Nido and to give the bears effective field protection until a long-term conservation plan could be drawn up and implemented. So far no financial support has been forthcoming, though the project is still on the active list.

Pending the implementation of some plan for grizzly protection, the Museum of Vertebrate Zoology has been compiling materials for a report on the ecology of the Sierra del Nido with emphasis on the vertebrate animals—mammals, birds, reptiles, and amphibians. If the area is ultimately to become a national park or wildlife refuge, reliable information on the fauna and flora will be useful. The fauna of this area is fascinating in itself, over and beyond the bear question. It draws elements from the Sierra Madre on the west, the lowland avifauna of Texas and eastern Mexico, and the temperate highlands

[4]The 1080 was supplied to the Panamerican Sanitary Board by the United States in a cooperative predator control program.—Eds.

both to the north and the south. Thus, among the birds one finds such diverse combinations as the orchard oriole and yellow-billed cuckoo associating with coppery-tailed and eared trogons, thick-billed parrots, wild turkeys, and Lucifer hummingbirds.

Of particular interest is the diversity and abundance of rattlesnakes. There are five distinct species—all of them abundant! One wonders how these different kinds and sizes of rattlers divide up the food resources without excessive competition. One of these—Willard's rattlesnake—is a truly beautiful animal with striking patterns of red shades, contrasted with white face markings. It was considered one of the rarest of all rattlesnakes until we found the big population in the Sierra del Nido.

Most of the big game mammals of north-central Mexico occur in the Sierra del Nido. White-tailed deer are abundant and a few prong-horn antelope frequent the foothills and llanos north of the Sierra. Wolves, black bears, and mountain lions still range the mountain in modest numbers; coyotes, bobcats, and gray foxes are all abundant. The bird and reptile faunas are rich and varied. This assortment of native animals, added to the rare attraction of the grizzly bear, ranks the area high in terms of faunal values. The issue which now faces conservationists, and the Mexican government, is whether these values can be preserved. Establishment of a national park or a national wildlife refuge would be a first step toward achieving this goal.

On Killing a Bear

David E. Brown

1982

Now it's time for the senior editor to tell his bear story.[1] That he is a biologist of long standing with the Arizona Game and Fish Department is unimportant. That he only wanted one bear and may never kill another may or may not be important. His motives and emotions are adequately stated in the text. What is significant is that he enjoyed himself and, in the process, became more enamored of bears than before. The ancient forces are still at work. ⚘

I don't remember when I decided to kill a bear. It must have been sometime in my youth, probably while reading a narration of a frontiersman's exploits. For whatever reason, I resolved to bag one someday. I just had to know what it meant to kill a bear.

Not any bear would do. It had to be an adult taken on its own terms. A female with a cub wouldn't do. I would not use a bait station or hire anyone with dogs to do the hunting for me. Stalking bear country with field glasses and a predator call became a hobby for almost twenty years. And I had my chances.

Several times I had seen bears—but too late in the day to make a

---

[1]An earlier version, entitled, "Brown's Bear Story," was published in the December 1982 issue of *Wildlife Views,* the Arizona Game and Fish Department magazine.

stalk and get in position. On two occasions I had spooked bears by
getting restless and giving up too soon. Both times I was offered only
a hasty shot at a retreating bruin some distance off. Having no desire
to wound a bear, I refrained from shooting. Both the bear and the
situation had to be right. Why not? There were plenty of oppor-
tunities.

One of the few advantages to living in Phoenix is its proximity to
bear country. Good bear populations are to be found in several
mountains within two hundred miles of the metropolis; on short
notice, one can be in reasonable bear habitat within two hours of
leaving home. Finding myself without either a deer permit or patrol
assignment on the opening weekend of deer season, I decided on an
impromptu hunt. For such occasions, I had a "honeyhole" only fifty
miles from my house.

I stopped at the 7-Eleven for coffee and a doughnut a little after
4:00 A.M., planning on being back that evening. I went alone, because there was no time to round up a suitable partner and because I
don't like to have to adjust my hunting to someone else's schedule.
The chances for encountering a bear on a one-day hunt were small,
but the important thing was to be out there. There's always a chance
of seeing a bear. Besides, I felt lucky.

The saguaros only grudgingly gave way to chaparral as I wound
my way up into the Mazatal Mountains. The U. S. Forest Service
road to El Oso Pass took longer to traverse than I had planned; by the
time I reached my destination the headlights were no longer needed. I
had missed the best time to glass for feeding bears. Even in late
October, no bear would be out past sunup.

It takes the better part of an hour to hike to the site where I had
once called in a big cinnamon bear and where I had vowed to try
again. The route is uphill, steep, and through dense manzanita and
other chaparral. Some of the brush had recently burned; some not.
The going was slow, for I took my time and moved as quietly as
conditions permitted. The trail to the old corral and spring eluded
me, but it didn't matter. I knew where I was. I felt keenly aware of my
surroundings. The wind was just right—a slight breeze drifting
downslope. No other hunters were to be seen, and I sensed a chance

for the perfect hunt. Even this late in the year there was an abundance of ripe prickly-pear fruit. Turbinella oak acorns and manzanita berries were on the bushes and on the ground. I stopped once to photograph prickly-pear apples and once to call.

No response. I slowly worked my way up to the saddle above the spring. That I saw no fresh bear sign bothered me not at all. Previous visits had told me that the other side of the ridge was where any bears would be in evidence. The important thing now was to make a stealthy approach—a feat that would have been more difficult if I had been accompanied by a partner.

I reached the destination for my appointed rendezvous. As I topped over to the north slope, the dense manzanita cover gave way to open glades of Gambel's oak and ponderosa pine. Inside the forest the going was quieter and the air cooler. Such open habitats are not used by bruin except at night, but my motive was to entice one out from the surrounding brush and make him visible. Almost immediately, I hit upon a well-used bear trail and followed it. Fresh tracks and droppings told me that a bear, or bears, were using the area— probably as recently as the previous night.

I quickly slid into my predetermined calling site. Here, near the crest of the ridge, a great Gambel's oak had fallen, making an excellent hiding place. Another large oak growing out of the debris of the dead monarch provided a backrest and shade. Sitting at the base of the standing tree, I relieved myself of my backpack and got comfortable.

The view through the forest was open enough to see for more than sixty yards in any direction. Only the faintest of breezes was now blowing—downslope and to my right. Sunlight filtered through the oak leaves, casting my surroundings in soft light and blotched shadows. My approach had been silent; an Arizona gray squirrel was rustling among the fallen leaves, searching for acorns and oblivious to my presence. Everything was perfect.

I squalled, then squeaked on my new "varmint call"—a gift for having made a presentation to a sportsmen's club in Mesa. Not quite satisfied with the tone of the reed, I went to using my old *Circe* call and made a few blows on it. Immediately several scrub jays came in, circling me with their raucous calls. Their persistence was extraordinary. The birds appeared more agitated than curious—their normal response to a predator call—and kept flying off somewhere and then returning. Something was up. I cradled my Model 70 and set the variable scope on 2.5, the lowest power. Peering intently through the foliage, I concentrated on where I had once seen a big whitetail buck and where I thought a bear might come.

It was then that I heard the growl—a growl heard only in the movies and never in the woods. Such a sound could come only from a bear. I glanced over my left shoulder in the unexpected direction from which the sound had come. What I saw was a huge bear bursting out of a manzanita thicket—not two dozen yards behind me—and coming.

I stood up instantly and put the gun to my shoulder, knowing as I did that he would see me and head for cover. No matter. He had committed himself, and I would get at least one shot at him before he disappeared back into the brush. Instead of spooking, though, he laid his ears back, and if anything, quickened his pace toward me. If ever I was going to shoot a bear, now was the time!

The scope was filled with bear. I sent the cross-hairs up his right leg to the shoulder, slid a tad over to his chest, and squeezed the trigger. The explosion was deafening. The bear visibly lurched from what I knew was a mortal wound. But he kept on.

I stood firm and found myself remarkably calm as the brute bounded downslope, flailing his massive forearms in front of him. Now coming directly at me, he presented a truly awesome sight. I barely had time to load a second round in the chamber—an action that, although instinctive, required dropping the gun from my shoulder to work the bolt. I have a left master eye and shoot left-handed.

The bear was upon me before I had time to reraise the rifle. Thrusting the muzzle out with my left hand, I fired into his head. The bear collapsed while I fell over backwards from the recoil.

The bear now lay at my feet, motionless and silent. Standing up, I touched an eye with the gun muzzle—not a blink or a quiver. A great exhilaration came over me and I couldn't believe my fortune. I had obtained a bear in the most classic fashion. I reached into my pack, removed my camera, and took several pictures "as he fell." The forest was as quiet as the bear.

I was excited now and somewhat shaken. My hands trembled as I secured the tag around his lower jaw—it wouldn't fit around the hind leg. I paced off the distance to where the bear had made his appearance—twenty-seven yards; to where I first shot it—twelve yards. For the first time I examined the bear closely. It was a big male with thick mahogany pelage, a magnificent specimen. His head was as big as the proverbial barrel, and the paws of large and wonderful size. Only the teeth were less than perfect. Broken tusks and worn molars indicated an animal past his prime.

As my adrenalin level receded, I began to realize the task in store for me. The bear must weigh close to 400 pounds; I could hardly move it and now regretted being alone. Not only could I use some help, but I wanted to show my prize to someone while it was still whole. The time was 10:30 in the morning.

The slope we were on was steep, so I propped the bear up with rocks to keep him from sliding downhill while I dressed him out. It took about a half-hour to remove the paunch and entrails. The animal was very fat and loaded with prickly-pear fruits from esophagus to anus. That job finished, I pulled out the lungs, heart, and liver, putting the latter two items in my pack. The first shot had gone through the lungs and severed the aorta. I had been right; the shot had been fatal. The bear just hadn't had time to know it.

It wasn't until I skinned out the first leg that I fully realized the chore facing me. My knife had grown dull and I had no hone in my pack. Rope, cord, and pack frame were also back in the truck. Unable to remove even one leg from the carcass, I decided to return to the truck and exchange my rifle, camera, binoculars, and day pack for a hone and pack frame. It was not yet noon and the weather was cool and crisp. Even dressed and in the shade, I still hated leaving bruin on the ground.

I tried to find a quicker route back to the truck but was unsuccessful; the trip still took an hour. En route, I had had time to think— why not get some help packing the bear out? I knew someone in

Tonto Basin who had a horse and who would probably help me. It would take all day today and tomorrow to get everything out by myself. Under no circumstances must the hide be allowed to spoil.

As luck would have it, I met a deer hunter on the road who took up my offer of half the meat if he would help pack it out. A husky truck driver, who had also been a butcher at some time in his career, he was a godsend, and he and his wife proved to be enthusiastic helpers. Still, it was late in the afternoon before we had the bear skinned, and well after dark when we stumbled back to our trucks with a front quarter apiece.

The next morning we returned for the hide and to bone out the remaining meat—back straps, shoulders, flanks, and so forth. The head and hide weighed close to 100 pounds and I staggered getting up under the load. Yet, I only remember stopping to rest on two occasions, both halfway up hills. In my mind, a rug in front of the fireplace was as good as there.

The head and hide were iced down and in Jack Wight's Taxidermy Studio by noon. The cape was in fine shape, and I was again impressed with what a fine animal I had. The back of the cranium had been blown out by the second round, so we couldn't score him for the Boone and Crockett record book. Too bad. He would have made it easily—at least the Arizona book.

Later I boiled out the skull and noted that the teeth were abscessed and badly decayed. Despite his bad teeth, the annual rings of the cementum indicated only a ten-year-old animal. Wild bears can live for up to twenty years or more. Was the bear cranky and aggressive or did he just not recognize the source of those enticing squeals? Experienced callers tell me the latter. Many a bear has come in with a rush to a predator call. Those planning to use such tactics had better keep in mind the animal's poor eyesight and plan accordingly. I must confess to a slight uneasiness at the thought of not having gotten off that second shot!

Old-time bear hunters—those from the South and those who hunt exclusively with hounds—tell an old wives' tale of "pig bears" and "dog bears." Dog bears have a long face, are lean and lanky, almost unfit to eat; pig bears are short of face, have a stocky build, and are excellent table fare. If such be so, I had me a "pig bear" whose meat made the best red chili burros I've ever eaten. Still, giving half to those fortuitous Samaritans was about the best deal I ever made.

I have no desire to possess another bear. One is enough. Those who tell of killing a dozen or more meet neither with my approval nor with my scorn. It's just that I have no reason to do so. I've already participated in the best hunt possible.

The Last
Southwestern Grizzly

John A. Murray

1986

While I have not hunted bears or killed bears myself, I have hunted them in the literature and in the far reaches of my mind. In this selection I describe a trip I made in 1986 to the location in the San Juan Mountains of Colorado where a female grizzly bear was killed in 1979. It is very likely that this individual specimen was the last grizzly bear in the American Southwest. Although there continue to be reports of grizzly bear activity in the South San Juans, nothing definite has been confirmed. Until the existence of other grizzlies in the region is indisputably verified, it must be assumed that the bear killed in 1979 was the last southwestern grizzly. Like "Martha," the last of the passenger pigeons that died in the Cincinnati Zoo in 1913, this grizzly was the last of her kind, a subspecies of bear that is now in all probability extinct. ✽

On August 9, 1986, deep in the San Juan Mountains of southwestern Colorado, I stood on the spot where the last grizzly in the Southwest was killed. To be more exact, I was probably within fifty yards of the location. The *precise* place may be forever lost. Official records never seem to be as accurate as we would like; in fact, they seem to be increasingly indefinite in direct proportion to the importance of the historical event they chronicle. There are, of course, no markers on the spot, nor will there ever be. Humankind does not build monuments to its mistakes. The only information about the site is found in a file cabinet drawer at the Denver Headquarters of the Colorado Division of Wildlife. I had with me on that day some relevant materials from that file: a photocopy of a 7.5-minute U.S.G.S. map and some field notes from the summary account of the September 23, 1979, incident. The map and notes indicated a timbered hillside slightly north and west of Blue Lake, a few yards south of the Continental Divide trail (or one of its several meandering branches), and just below a conspicuous prominence at an altitude of about 11,600 feet.

I did the best I could and finally settled on a likely piece of deadfall probably within a few yards of where she was killed. The field photograph of the bear carcass showed her piled up against a dead tree. It was late in the day and the forest of spruce and fir was solemn and quiet, almost melancholy, as the cloudy skies to the west began to darken with an approaching hailstorm. A cold wind swept in off the Divide, and the tree tops began to sway back and forth, moaning in a low mournful tone. Even in August the weather can be severe at timberline, and I knew I didn't have much time before the storm struck. I sat back against the spruce deadfall, sheltered from the wind, and reflected on the events that had brought me to such a remote and lonely location on what was, back in the flat country of Denver, a pleasant summer day.

Ever since researching the chapter on grizzly bears for my book *Wildlife in Peril: The Endangered Mammals of Colorado* (Roberts Rinehart, 1987), I had been intrigued with the idea of visiting, of making a sort of pilgrimage, to the place where the last grizzly in the Southwest was killed. It would, I had realized, require a special physical effort and commitment of time. Blue Lake is one of the more inaccessible glacial cirques in the San Juan Mountains. To get there from Denver requires a six- or seven-hour drive through South Park and the San Luis Valley, and then a twelve-mile hike from the trailhead near the confluence of the South Fork and the Main Fork of the Conejos River. But it seemed to me that several valuable things could be achieved during the trip. I knew, for example, that I would be able to see up close the sort of habitat that the bears require in order to live in the contemporary West. I could also consider the death of the grizzly not as an end but as a beginning, and the visit could become an important part of that beginning. Finally, hiking through some beautiful country I had wanted to explore, not to mention fishing some premier wild water, was always sufficient reason for such an outing.

I was jarred out of my musing as the first hailstones rattled through the evergreen boughs.

I pulled a wool sweater and poncho from my day pack and battened down the hatches. The storm struck the high isolated ridge with all its fury: wave after wave of hailstones poured down on the forest and bolts of lightning exploded on the prominence behind me like impacting artillery rounds. Dry and warm beneath my poncho, I pulled out my lunch and waited for the storm to pass. Forty minutes later, the hail turned to rain and, after a short while, the rain stopped, the clouds began to break up, and the sun came out, blazing down on an alpine world suddenly turned white from hail piled ankle-deep. I walked through the forest, filled now with white slush, and stopped at the cliffs, where I had a spectacular view looking down the headwaters of the Navajo River into southern Colorado and northern New Mexico. The air, the mountains, and the canyon of the upper Navajo were fresh and cleanly washed. Everything sparkled in the sunlight. Across the canyon nearly a mile away I could see individual snowbanks and Douglas firs as clearly as if they were just up the slope.

What most impressed me about the scene, though, was that it was some of the best bear habitat I've ever seen. On either side of the canyon, steep avalanche chutes, holding berries, roots, leaves, and rodents, were interspersed among spruce-fir stringers. At the bottom of the canyon, as narrow and white as streamers of Christmas tree tinsel, was the Navajo River, and, all around it, were the boggy meadows and beaver ponds—the wet acreage—so prized by bears. In the forest and parks above were herds of elk and deer. Far below, and at much lower elevations, were the necessary components of *spring range*, the area where bears find vital food sources after emerging from the den.

Grizzlies have long lived in the area. In April 1913, hunter William Wieseel killed three grizzlies on the lower Navajo. Other bears were killed in the region in the following decades. In 1951, sheepherder Al Lobato killed a young grizzly at Blue Lake. Its head, mounted by Ernie Wilkinson (who in September of that year also killed a grizzly to the north near Rio Grande Reservoir) can still be seen at the Platoro Lodge. The next summer government hunter and trapper Lloyd Anderson killed a grizzly at the headwaters of the Los Pinos River, also to the north. Two cubs reportedly escaped. Perhaps one of those cubs was the grizzly killed by Ed Wiseman at Blue Lake on September 23, 1979.

As I stood there I noticed a coyote crossing a meadow beneath the cliffs. It, too, had found some shelter from the storm, for its dusky summer coat was dry. Perhaps it had a rock den in the talus slide nearby, or it had found refuge under the heavy boughs of a spruce. It veered off downslope, heading for some wide grass meadows, where, no doubt, the mice hunting was good. The coyote, like the mountain lion and the black bear, still inhabits the San Juans. The larger gray wolf and grizzly bear do not. All were subjected to intense persecution in the form of unlimited trapping, hunting, and poisoning in the first half of the twentieth century. For reasons that are still not completely understood, the first three managed to survive, while the last two were extirpated.

I wandered around the headwaters of the Navajo until the sun disappeared behind the gathering black clouds of a second storm. This storm threatened to be even more intense than the first. In my wanderings, I found many signs of bears: scats, scratch trees, digging sites, even a fairly recent day bed, dug into an old elk day bed behind a Douglas fir with a commanding view of the back trail. But I found no sign of El Oso Plateado. At least none that was readily recognizable. Perhaps there are still some silvertips left in the South San Juans, but I doubt it. Even if there are, it will take restoration, not preservation, to ensure that a viable population endures. Until further evidence is forthcoming, we must assume the grizzly killed by Wiseman was the last grizzly in Colorado, and, in all probability, the last grizzly in the Southwest.

The Wiseman grizzly, as it has become known, met its end in a bizarre and controversial incident during the archery elk season in

1979. Although there is much dispute as to the veracity of the story told by the participants, the account is worth relating from a historical standpoint. Ed Wiseman, a burly forty-six-year-old outfitter, was, on that fateful autumn afternoon, guiding Mike Niederee of Great Bend, Kansas, on an elk hunt. The two were still hunting with bows and arrows in the timber at the Navajo River headwaters. This is a good area to hunt elk, because the 77,000-acre Banded Peak Ranch just to the south is managed as a wildlife refuge, and hunting around its edges can be profitable for trophy hunters. In fact, it is likely the grizzly survived in part because her home range was largely on that ranch.

At around five in the evening Niederee claims to have jumped a bear in its day bed. Despite being surprised at close distance, the bear chose to avoid a confrontation and fled the scene. Several hundred yards away it ran into Wiseman, and, according to their deposition, that is when the trouble began. The bear reportedly knocked Wiseman down and began to maul him. At first Wiseman tried to remain passive and appear dead, a strategy recommended in bear attacks. This, however, did not seem to work, and growing desperate, he grabbed a hunting arrow and began to stab the bear in the throat and neck. The bear, weakened by injuries, released Wiseman, lumbered off into the twilight, and died a short distance away.

Niederee, alerted by Wiseman's cries, arrived on the scene to find the outfitter a bloody mess. Wiseman had suffered several bites, a broken right leg, a mangled foot, and considerable blood loss in the attack. After applying what first aid he could, Niederee left to get the horses, which were tied off about one mile over the ridge. He returned with them, but Wiseman was in such bad shape that he could not be moved. Niederee made a large fire, gathered plenty of kindling, and, as the cold and darkness settled on the high mountains, left for Wiseman's hunting base camp on the North Fork of the Conejos River. Several hours later Niederee arrived at the base camp. The camp cook rode out to the trailhead for help, while the rest of the party, including Niederee's father, a surgeon, rode back over the Divide to Wiseman, reaching him about four in the morning. The rescue party rebuilt the fire and attended to his wounds. Wiseman had lost a lot of blood and was now, in addition to his injuries, suffering from hypothermia. A helicopter evacuated him from the site later that morning. He eventually recovered from the attack and returned to outfitting. He was still maintaining a hunting camp on the North Fork above Platoro Reservoir, in the 1980s.

A later helicopter flight removed the grizzly bear skull and hide from the site, but left the bear's carcass behind. This was a substantial loss to science, as a close examination of the uterus for placental scars could have determined if the bear had ever borne cubs—evidence that other grizzlies might still reside in the area. A number of biologists who later examined the pelt agreed that the pigmentation and enlargement of the mammaries strongly suggested that the grizzly had nursed cubs in the past.

The Colorado Division of Wildlife conducted a two-year study of the South San Juans (1980–1982), and found only possible evidence of grizzlies in the area: a number of large digging sites, a partially collapsed grizzly bear den, and a possible sighting of a blond-phased adult female with two dark cubs. The last sighting was particularly intriguing because biologists found a large number of dig sites and a quantity of long blond bear hairs at that location. Black bears are generally thought to be unable to undertake large digs, as do grizzlies, because of their much shorter foreclaws. Because of the large size of the study area, the reclusiveness of grizzlies, the large number of black bears, and the ruggedness of the region, the results were inconclusive. While some officials concede that a bear or two might still remain in the mountains, there are no management plans for the grizzly at present, and none planned.

The death of the Wiseman grizzly is, in a larger sense, emblematic of so much of what we are doing to the planet. One by one, plant and animal species are disappearing as their habitat is invaded or attenuated by humankind. Even in the remote South San Juans, there is extensive livestock grazing, high intensity recreational use, logging, mining, and winter ski activities. It is incredible the bear survived so long. Perhaps even more remarkable is that the last grizzly was not killed in the Sierra Madres, the Mogollons, or the Sierra Del Nidos, but in the San Juans of Colorado, a state that has experienced unprecedented growth since 1970. The tenacity, courage, and intelligence of this magnificent animal are surely deserving of our admiration.

I keep a photograph of the Navajo River headwaters above my desk to look at when the snows are deep. I think of the summer day high in the San Juan Mountains when the memory of a grizzly led me to a wild and beautiful location. The site is worthy of an epitaph: *Here one species, persecuted by another species, became extinct.* It would be even more of a tribute to the bear if we took that incident not as an excuse to declaim the past, but rather as an inspiration to redress the mistakes of the past and to restore the grizzly to the Southwest.

Epilogue

WHEREAS, the growth of the human population has impinged upon the habitat needed by the grizzly bear and the gray (timber) wolf within Colorado, and

WHEREAS, any introduction of wolves or grizzly bear is potential conflict with huntable species of wildlife, the livestock industry, and the human welfare, and

WHEREAS, a population of gray (timber) wolves or grizzly bear introduced into Colorado could become a management problem, when not contained within its designated management area, and

WHEREAS, biological control of big game herds through predation is not feasible, and

WHEREAS, the human welfare, and the value of Colorado's livestock and wildlife resources is of considerable importance,

NOW THEREFORE BE IT RESOLVED, that the Colorado Wildlife Commission hereby establishes and declares its opposition to every person or entity which may now or in the future suggest or plan the introduction of either the gray (timber) wolf or the grizzly bear as free-roaming populations within the State of Colorado.

Resolution unanimously adopted
by the Colorado Wildlife
Commission, January 1982

Headwaters of the Navajo River, San Juan Mountains, Colorado—locale of the Southwest's last grizzly population. Photograph by John A. Murray.

I keep returning to Antonito, Colorado. I shouldn't; it's not in my sphere of influence and usually out of the way to where I'm going. But something keeps drawing me there whenever crane viewing, grouse hunting, or other excuses cause me to travel north to the Rocky Mountain Empire. Maybe its because, as an Arizonan, I find the Mexican population of that hamlet reassuring. Its overwhelming Hispanic character means that I am now safely ensconced within the Southwest.

Finding myself there while returning from the sharp-tailed grouse country around Steamboat Springs one autumn, I decided to do something different. Instead of continuing south to Santa Fe, I would follow State Highway 17 west along the Conejos River to Chama. The Conejos's undammed floodplain and superb stands of narrowleaf cottonwoods were an irresistible appeal and a refreshing reminder of what *rillitos* should look like. And so, I followed the river upstream to take in the mountains of north-central New Mexico and the historic

Cumbres and Toltec Narrow-gauge Railroad before returning home to Arizona from New Mexico.

The stream tumbled forward to meet me—the shimmering canary yellow of the September cottonwoods erratically reflected in its waters. Before long each switchback presented a vista of exhilarating beauty. The varied greens of the conifer-clad watershed were punctuated by swatches of aspens cast in gold and coppery pink. I pulled over to take in the colors and touch the breezes of late afternoon.

I was not alone. A pickup camper was also parked on the gravel turnout. Two hunters were glassing for elk in preparation for the coming season. Seeing me staring off into the forest, they assumed that I was of like persuasion. They told me what great elk country this was and where past herds had been seen and kills made. As an aside they confided to me that this was also good bear country.

Of course! It now dawned on me that what I was looking at was the south side of the San Juan Mountains—some of the best bear habitat anywhere. If I were to hike up the divide that we were glassing, I would come to Platoro Lake, the death site of the Southwest's last grizzly. Immediately the landscape took on new excitement. This was not only "bear country"; it was Grizzly Country—or had been up until just recently.

And it wasn't so long ago that wolves were present, too. In 1927 a small pack had crossed over the San Juans from Colorado into New Mexico to terrorize the Carson National Forest before a two-year effort by ranchers and the U. S. Biological Survey eradicated these last holdouts. The animals might have even crossed through the same defile that now held my attention. Well, they wouldn't be there now. The animals eliminated in 1928 were the last Rocky Mountain wolves in the Southwest. My exhilaration turned to outrage and then contemplation. What right had the government to deprive me of a legacy of wolves and grizzlies on the public domain?

I knew the answer as well as anyone. It wasn't a matter of right but a desire to please. The men who had eradicated the wolf and the grizzly were not especially selfish or arrogant; on the contrary, they were attempting to do good. Who could have foreseen then that "big bears" and *lobos* would someday have a value other than the skewed

respect of those who hunted them? No, there was no point in villify-
ing the men who single-mindedly went about their business of elimination. Their intention was only to make the West a fit place to raise
stock and to help the Forest Service become compatible with western
mores. How were they to know that everything would change—that
elk and defunct railways would be more valuable commodities than
either sheep or cattle?

The thought of wolves, grizzlies, or both having thwarted their
programmed extermination amused me. If either of these cumbersome predators had done so, the San Juans would now be a great
study area, the object and site of symposia of scientists, the subject of
reams of management plans, and the beneficiary of enormous sums
squandered on ways to preserve their canine and ursine refugees in
the face of "historic" land uses and modern "developments."

But neither species survived. Like the jaguar, the wolf and the
grizzly were destroyed to leave the field to the more elusive cougar.
To return either of these "big" carnivores will require overt action.
And why not bring them back? Would not a government that spends
millions on Masked Bobwhite, Black-footed Ferrets, and California
Condors want to return such celebrated species as bears and wolves to
their ancestoral haunts on government land?

The answer is no. Not if it's up to government administrators.
Their watchword could well be "millions for remnants, but not one
cent for reintroductions"—at least as far as controversial carnivores
are concerned. For them, there is a big difference between preservation and restoration; one is politically acceptable, but the other is not.

Must this state of affairs continue indefinitely? Might not the U. S.
Fish and Wildlife Service, the U. S. Forest Service, and the state
Game and Fish departments be *too* reactive to what is perceived as
trouble to be avoided? In the case of the wolf, probably not.

Releasing wolves could generate a conflict with the livestock industry that would be so venomous as to preclude sustained public
support for further reintroduction programs. The wide-ranging wolf
is too inefficient a predator on native game to pass up man's smor-
gasbord of beef, veal, lamb, and mutton. It is no accident that Amer-

ica's remaining wolves are all in boreal habitats too severe for the year-long pasturing of bovine and ovine nuisances. No, the time for the wolf's return to the Southwest has not yet come, if it ever does.

Such does not have to be the case for the Great Bear. Conflicts would exist, to be sure, but I believe that such disputes could be made manageable if the resolve to succeed is strong. There are new management techniques that would minimize the potential for depredations and increase the grizzly's chances to survive. Let's look at the bear's real and implied threat to livestock first.

Although a number of U. S. Forest Service allotments would feasibly have to be "retired" from grazing for use by grizzlies, there is little question but that a bear with wanderlust would eventually take a sheep or a cow. Unlike the wolf, however, depredation on cattle need not be chronic and need no longer be exacerbated, as in the past, by livestock preempting the bear's spring forage. Transplanting only bears without stock-killing experience would also reduce the potential for depredation. And failing all else, the budget for such a program should contain a proviso reimbursing ranchers for legitimate losses resulting from transplanted grizzlies. Indeed, I believe that, if properly planned, a transplant program could have a quiet truce with the ranching community and might even be tacitly encouraged by some cattlemen. The area selected for such a venture should be large, in good historic grizzly country, and too rough to be good for cattle grazing. An established or *de facto* wilderness managed primarily for wildlife would be ideal.

What about the threat of grizzlies to humans? Unlike wolves, grizzlies do occasionally kill people. The last death by grizzly in the Southwest was Hyrum Naegle in 1892, the eyewitness account of which is included in this anthology. As with all of the region's few deaths by grizzlies that I am aware of, the "attack" was by a wounded bear. Unprovoked attacks in areas having a low-density population of grizzlies are a threat more imagined than real. Even if a hiker should be waylaid, southwestern forests harbor far greater dangers. More people have been killed falling over waterfalls in the Coronado National Forest in southern Arizona than have been killed by bears in all of the country's national forests combined! The possible attack of a grizzly is something we will have to accept if we are to preserve this semblance of our frontier heritage.

But even if we have become a nation of wimps so tame that life is valued more than living, there is an alternative solution. Import European brown bears. These shy creatures are the same species and size as the native grizzly, *Ursus arctos,* but with 2,000 more years of fending off civilization under their belts, they have become habituated by evolutionary process to getting along with Man. For instance, no one in Italy can remember anyone ever being attacked by a bear in that country of 55,000,000 people and 150 bears. Yugoslavia, Greece, Spain, France, Norway, and other European countries share a similar experience.

We already have large areas set aside to preserve the frontier. The San Juans are just one example, and perhaps not the best place to reintroduce grizzlies—too many sheep still in the vicinity. The Blue Primitive Area in Arizona and the Gila and Aldo Leopold wilderness areas in New Mexico might be better. A survey of potential sites would certainly be an early priority in any reintroduction effort.

An important ingredient may be the attitude of a particular Forest Service Supervisor or Game and Fish Department Director. Politics will probably be a more decisive factor than biological considerations. All of the Southwest states contain designated and *de facto* wilderness areas formerly held by good populations of grizzly that are now managed to retain their wilderness character, if not a wilderness fauna. In the Gila, livestock leases have already been retired in deference to wildlife. Wilderness is more than the heritage of these places—it is their future. And a mountain fastness without grizzlies is like a desert mountain range without bighorns—incomplete.

There will always be a plethora of reasons why grizzlies can't be introduced. Reluctance of public land administrators and the possibility of tort claims won't be the only hurdles. The mere prospect that such a program could fail will deter some. Others will object to using any stock other than what they perceive as the race historically present. Such "purists" will demand that any Southwest experiment hold out for "Mexican grizzlies."

Such talk is academic in the truest sense. There are no Mexican grizzlies—none to transplant, anyway. Beside, the San Juans, Gila, and White mountains are more Rocky Mountain than Madrean—an observation that goes back to Bartlett's day. Montana or Wyoming bears will do just fine, maybe even British Columbia or other Holarctic bears. No one today objects to the fact that the elk now doing so well in Arizona and New Mexico all came from Wyoming!

The recent development of new capture and immobilization techniques allows for some innovative approaches and should alleviate some concerns. Stocking only mother grizzlies who are known homebodies—females that have a reputation for avoiding Man and cattle—is one idea. Another proposed technique is to adopt grizzly cubs to hibernating black bear mothers. Again, only the best adapted bears with a reputation for secretive behavior and successful cub-raising would be used as surrogates. No "garbage bears" or "stock-killers," please. Over time, a population of grizzlies as trouble-free as those in Italy or Yugoslavia might be realized. Why not give it a try?

"See any elk?" the man asked. Jarred out of my daydreams about grizzlies, I blithered a response. "No," I said. "I was looking for something else; something not there yet." He looked at me strangely—like I might be a bit addled. Maybe he was right. I would like to see bruin returned to his high country home. A southwesterner shouldn't have to go to Alaska, Montana, or Europe to see a silvertip. Not with all the wilderness we have in bear country. President Theodore Roosevelt and Aldo Leopold didn't establish National Forests and Wilderness Areas to make America safe; they wanted to preserve a semblance of the frontier's adventure.

DAVID E. BROWN was employed by the Arizona Game and Fish Department for twenty-five years as a Wildlife Manager, Big Game Management Supervisor, and Game Branch Supervisor. His book, *The Grizzly in the Southwest,* was published by the University of Oklahoma Press in 1984. Other published works include *The Wolf in the Southwest* and *Arizona's Wetlands and Waterfowl,* both in print with the University of Arizona Press. His search to learn more about bears has taken him into almost every mountain range in the Southwest and from Montana to Abruzzo National Park in Italy.

JOHN A. MURRAY, an instructor in the English Department at the University of Denver, is the author of four nature books: *The Indian Peaks Wilderness Area* (1985), *Wildlife in Peril: The Endangered Mammals of Colorado* (1987), *The Gila Wilderness Area* (1988), and *The South San Juan Wilderness Area* (1988). He has completed a series of essays on the national parks and has begun exploring the relationship between wilderness and the American consciousness in the twentieth century.